DATE DUE

SEP 3 1980	AUG 1 4 1985	MAY 2 0 2000
APR 2 9 1981	OCT 2 2 1986	OCT 1 8 2000
APR 2 8 1982	SEP 3 1987	MAR 2 1 2001
AUG 1 8 1982	DEC 2 3 1989	AUG 1 5 2001
FEB 1 6 1988	AUG 2 1993	
JUL 6 - 1983	MAR 2 7 1995	
JUN 2 7 1984	AUG 2 2 1995	
OCT 2 4 1984	OCT 1 6 1995	

PURE MAGIC!

PURE MAGIC!

THE SLEIGHT-OF-HAND BOOK OF DAZZLING TRICKS AND CAPTIVATING ROUTINES

HENRY GROSS

Charles Scribner's Sons
NEW YORK

Copyright © 1978 Henry Gross

Library of Congress Cataloging in Publication Data
Gross, Henry—
    Pure magic.
    1. Conjuring.   I. Title.
GV1555.G74   793.8   77-15069
ISBN 0-684-15338-6

1 3 5 7 9 11 13 15 17 19 M/C 20 18 16 14 12 10 8 6 4 2

Printed in the United States of America

For Monique

CONTENTS

INTRODUCTION

The modern magician assumes many guises. He may stride
the stage as a flamboyant illusionist in a scarlet cloak, or deftly
manipulate a deck of cards at a shipboard table, or pose as a
"psychic" who guesses birthdays, reads sealed letters, and
bends spoons. He may escape from locked trunks, produce
doves from the air, or saw girls in half, but no matter what his
specialty, you can be sure that he is grounded in the fun-
damentals of sleight of hand.

I believe that if you want to perform magic you should
begin by learning sleight of hand rather than the so-called
easy tricks described in many books and available at all magic
shops. Although sleight of hand takes practice, the satisfaction
to be derived from learning it and the effects that can be
produced with it more than compensate for the effort. Once
you have mastered basic sleights you can perform startling
and entertaining close-up magic for family and friends and
add endlessly to your repertoire. You will have an absorbing
hobby that will bring you—and others—pleasure throughout
your life. If your ambition and talent so dictate, you can eventually graduate to larger magic more suitable for the stage.

This is a guide to performing basic sleight of hand with the
objects magicians have traditionally found best suited for ma-

nipulation—coins, playing cards, balls of various sizes and materials, silk handkerchiefs, and ribbons. These objects are used unprepared; the magic is performed by sleight of hand alone.

The book is divided into chapters devoted to these objects. Generally I explain the basic sleights that can be done with the object and then describe tricks, or routines, as they are often called, that depend on the application of the sleights. The tricks represent only a sampling of the large and varied repertoire of close-up magic that has come down through the years.

Today's close-up magician is a far cry from the parlor magician of yesteryear. Gone are the days when an audience would sit patiently in an overheated room while an overstuffed magician arranged his gold-fringed tables and cumbersome props. As the pace of life has speeded up, so has the pace of magic. Magicians must confront audiences accustomed to the rapid movement of events on television, whose attention span has shrunk and whose threshold of boredom is low. Interminable card tricks and clumsy apparatus are obsolete. Modern close-up magic must be impromptu and fast-paced. This is the kind of magic I have included in this book.

Assuming that most readers will perform for small audiences at social gatherings, I have included only tricks that are effective at close range and that need only a bare minimum of paraphernalia. In fact, everything you need to perform the magic in this book can be found around the house or in the dime store.

In keeping with my conviction that magic ought to be impromptu, I have included tricks that need no preparation before performance. As an amateur magician, you will perform in circumstances where there is no time for preparation. You must be able to produce magic on the spot.

As I have already hinted, this kind of magic requires practice. It doesn't come easily. But before you return the book and ask for your money back, consider this: you spend only a fraction of your time performing; the rest, practicing. If you don't enjoy practicing, there's not much point in choosing magic as a hobby. Practicing magic *is* enjoyable, as I think you will find once you begin. In learning a new sleight or routine, you are solving problems and overcoming obstacles, and for many people this can be quite exhilarating. Once you have mastered the rudiments, you will be exercising your imagination as you experiment with different ways of performing a new routine. In that sense, magic is an extremely creative pastime. It is also a voyage of discovery full of suspense and excitement; the search for new sleights and routines in books and magazines is a veritable treasure hunt, even though the prize is impalpable. Regard practice as a pleasure, not a chore, and you will make rapid progress.

When you practice magic, don't be impatient if at first you have difficulty in learning a sleight. There is a breakthrough point in learning every sleight, so don't get discouraged before it comes. Repeat the moves over and over, regardless of how bad you think they look. The muscles learn slowly, but they have an intelligence of their own. Suddenly, the knowledge acquired during hours of repetition will bear fruit; the breakthrough will occur and you will find that you have mastered the sleight.

Practice in front of a mirror, but don't become dependent on the glass. Use the mirror to see the effect from the audience's viewpoint, then break away and practice before an imaginary audience. If you practice exclusively before a mirror you will become accustomed to gauging your movements solely by your reflection, and when you are suddenly confronted by an audience you will feel lost.

Of course, practicing leads to performing, where the manual technique developed in solitude must stand up to public scrutiny. However, manual technique in itself is not enough to hold and entertain an audience. A magician must master the art of presentation. This all-important aspect of magic is covered in the first chapter, perhaps the most important in the book. It is here that I explain the psychological factors that play an essential part in deceiving an audience and the theatrical techniques that raise deception to the level of entertainment. While manual skill can be developed by practice, only performing can teach you the art of presentation. There is no substitute for working before an audience, noting their responses, and gauging their credulity.

Finally, here are two rules that every magician obeys, and I strongly suggest that you conform to the custom:

1. Never repeat a trick.
2. Never explain how a trick is done.

The first rule is not rigid; there are a few tricks that profit from repetition. Usually, though, a bit of the mystery is lost the second time. Your audience will often try to coax you into repeating a trick, but resist the temptation.

The second rule is based not so much on the need to guard the secrets of magic but on the need to protect the audience from disappointment. Most of the secrets of magic are quite simple. After all, you are only producing the *illusion* of magic, not the real thing. Yet the audience, on the deepest level, prefers to believe in the illusion. It is better not to rob them of this belief. They prefer to wonder.

Let them wonder.

1/ The Presentation of Magic

There is a popular notion about magic that is often expressed in the phrase "The hand is quicker than the eye." This suggests that a magician produces his effects by sleight of hand alone. In fact, sleight of hand is only one aspect of the magician's art. Of equal importance is the collection of techniques grouped under the heading of "presentation."

What does a close-up magician do? He stands or sits before an audience and tells them a little story, illustrated with the props of his choosing—a pack of cards, a few coins, a silk handkerchief. The conclusion of the story is always the same: magic. The objects behave in ways that contradict our expectations—and the laws of physics. They vanish or appear, change, multiply, penetrate solid matter. In performing these little stories or plays, the magician becomes something of an actor—an old-style actor who addresses his audience directly. His manner of "acting" the trick is what is meant by presentation.

Pretense

At the heart of the art of acting is the ability to pretend. Without this ability, one cannot act in a play. After all, the actor is asked to imagine that he is someone else, in an imaginary situation, on a stage or set that is obviously unreal—yet he must involve himself in these fictional circumstances and behave as if they *were* real.

The magician is not faced with such a demanding task. But in presenting his tricks—his plays—he is also pretending, and he must try to be as convincing as possible.

The first step in building conviction into the presentation of magic is to practice important sleights three ways. Let us take the coin pass, the first sleight in the book, as an example. This sleight involves pretending to place the coin in one hand while actually retaining it palmed in the other, then showing that the coin has vanished from the hand into which it was apparently placed. Here are the three steps in learning this sleight.

1. Practice the fake transfer, as described in the text, a few times until you get the feel of it. Observe your behavior in the mirror.

2. Now, with the same moves required to perform the fake transfer, execute a real transfer—that is, actually place the coin in the other hand. Again, observe your behavior in the mirror. Note whenever the real transfer resembles the fake transfer.

3. Practice the fake transfer and try to imitate the real transfer as closely as possible.

That is how the physical truth of a sleight is obtained. But there is another phase in perfecting this coin vanish. While practicing the moves, try to *imagine* that the coin is actually in the empty hand, and forget about its being palmed. Try to remember what it felt like to have the cool coin in your closed hand; this will help you to imagine it is there. When the time comes to perform the sleight in public, forget about everything and just do it. Act out the pass but don't get bogged down in imagining a nonexistent coin. The work you have done in rehearsal will carry over into your performance.

The example of the coin pass illustrates the element of belief that must be present in all good magic. It is unnecessary to practice every move in the manner just described, but it is important to develop naturalness and conviction in whatever you do. You must act the pretense of the trick with as much belief as you can summon. Otherwise, no matter how skillful you are, the audience will not fully believe you.

Always keep in mind what you are pretending to do, what the audience is supposed to believe. Often, beginners actually lose the main thrust of a trick and become confused, and their hands go totally out of control. For example, in teaching the coin pass to students, I have observed that they forget the point: that they have pretended to place a coin in one hand. They close the hand for a moment, but because there is nothing *in* there, because they don't actually *believe* in that nonexistent coin, they allow the hand to open, while they close the hand that palms the coin. Of course, the trick then makes no sense.

Work for plausibility in all your moves. If the routine demands turning your side to the audience, or dropping your hand into your lap, or moving an object from one side of the table to the other, find some reason for doing it. Be authentic in your behavior and your audience will believe your magic.

Patter

Although many stage magicians perform silently, to music, the close-up magician usually talks to his audience. This talk is called patter, an extremely important part of presentation.

Patter has basically three purposes: (1) to explain to the spectators what you are doing so they can follow the trick and appreciate the conclusion; (2) to direct the attention of the audience away from the action (misdirection), allowing you secretly to accomplish a vital move; (3) to entertain the audience and keep their interest alive.

Early books on magic instructed the student to write out his patter and memorize it. For the close-up magician, this is unnecessarily restrictive. Patter cannot be created independently of action. You must first learn the manual part of a trick and then match the patter to it.

Patter may be nothing more than a running description of the trick, or it may be a humorous story that uses the props in the trick as characters, or something in between. The idea is to find the particular peculiarity of a trick and to create a patter that expresses it. For example, in the cut and restored ribbon (Chapter 16), it is necessary to form a special loop in order to cut the ribbon properly for a later restoration. The ribbon reminded me of wrapping gifts at Christmas time, and the loop was like the bow with which you usually finish a package. And so I created a patter that revolves around the problem of wrapping gifts and inadvertently cutting the ribbon in the wrong place. On the other hand, certain tricks are so strong in themselves that they need only a sparse verbal accompaniment to explain what you are doing. The spongeball routine (Chapter 7) falls into this group.

Magic is essentially funny. You will discover this when you begin performing. When you violate the laws of physics and cause objects to behave in ways that contradict the expectations of the audience, the reaction will be laughter. This laughter is so joyful and spontaneous that you should always encourage it. Push the humor of magic to its limits. Now, this will depend to a large extent on how funny a person you naturally are. If you have a natural gift for comedy, you will be that much better a magician, for humor is entertaining, and magic ought to be as entertaining as possible.

This does not mean that you ought to pepper your show with a lot of corny jokes and sight gags. Let the humor in magic emerge naturally, but help it along with witty patter whenever you can. And if you can do a double take or a comical turn, don't hold back. You are there to entertain the audience, and when you hear laughter you know that you are succeeding.

The best way to compose patter is to find the general theme during rehearsal and to create a rough script in your mind as you work. As you perfect the trick, you will find yourself enriching the patter with new ideas. But don't set it. Rather, allow yourself the freedom to improvise during performance. All kinds of things happen during a performance, including mistakes, and you must feel free to ad-lib when necessary. If patter is set too rigidly, you are apt to be at a loss for words if you make a mistake or are interrupted.

One of the essential qualities in an actor's performance is spontaneity—the ability to create the illusion that what the audience is seeing on the stage (or on film) is happening for the first time. Indeed, teachers of acting refer to "the illusion of the first time." Actors achieve this by allowing themselves the freedom to respond freshly every night to the other actors in the play, letting new gestures and nuances of speech occur spontaneously.

A magician, too, must keep his effects fresh and create the illusion of the first time. He can do this only if he leaves room for improvised gestures and bits of patter, playing off the audience whenever possible, responding to the various personalities in every group. Every time you perform a trick, try to do it a little differently. This will give it freshness and the illusion that you are actually creating a miracle—for the first time—before the eyes of the spectators.

The main reason for difficulty with patter is that the magician has not thoroughly learned the trick that it accompanies. In order to speak freely and fluently—perhaps humorously—you must practice a routine until the moves become so automatic that no thought is required to execute them. Since it is difficult for the mind to concentrate on two things simultaneously, it cannot attend adequately to both the manual part of a trick and the verbal accompaniment. Both will suffer. But if through practice the chain of manual actions has become automatic, the mind can concentrate on speech.

Style and Dress

When I took up magic, in the late thirties, I acquired the catalog of a dealer and pored over it for more hours than I ever devoted to a schoolbook. (Like the skillful pool player, the adept amateur magician can also say that his accomplishments are a sign of a misspent youth!) I could have described the effect and quoted the price of every trick in the catalog. What I especially liked were the drawings of magicians that illustrated the tricks. They were dressed in tailcoat and top hat and had curling little moustaches and pointed goatees.

This character, a hangover from the late nineteenth century, continues to haunt modern magic. But despite his persistence in the public mind, there has been a healthy development in the evolution of magical style.

The Magic Show, a musical comedy with a magic show embedded in its core, opened on Broadway over three years ago and is still running as this book goes to press. The story concerns a small nightclub in the suburbs of New Jersey which features a magician in its floor show. The magician gets drunk and fails to show up for his performance, and so the manager hires another magician, sight unseen, through a New York agent. When he arrives, there is great consternation, for this magician doesn't look like a magician. He looks like a hippie. He wears a pair of tight, bell-bottomed jeans and a T-shirt, and his hair qualifies him for membership in the cast of another recent musical.

Meanwhile, the first magician returns, hung over and haggard but bent on keeping his job. The two present a stark contrast in magical 'styles. The first magician is conventionally dressed in tailcoat and top hat. He struts and preens, he boasts and bellows. He is a pompous bore. The newcomer, originally played by Doug Henning, who was recently replaced by Joseph Abaldo, is modest and low-key. He has broken from the traditional stereotype in which his colleague is imprisoned and has found an original style that suits his personality.

Now, I'm not suggesting that formal dress should be banned from magicdom. Certain magicians fit perfectly into a tailcoat; their personalities are tailored to the outfit. Cardini was one notable example of a magician whose formal dress became the trademark of his style. My only point is that formal dress is not the *only* permissible costume.

As a close-up magician, you do not have to be concerned with questions of costume, but you will be fumbling toward some kind of style. The search for a style is one of the challenging aspects of learning magic.

Of course, you can simply be yourself and perform your tricks in a natural manner. Naturalness is essential in close-up magic. Never disguise yourself behind a false personality.

There is another dimension to being yourself, though, and I suggest that you consider it. It is possible to use a *part* of yourself that performing brings to the surface. Our personalities are composed of many parts. We behave differently with different people, in different situations. As a student magician, you should feel free to allow certain feelings, a part of your personality that may otherwise remain hidden, to emerge before an audience.

Sometimes it is necessary to change your style to fit the occasion. At college I performed at a bazaar which was held in the gym. I worked in a booth, and the spectators would gather across the counter, in small groups, for five-minute shows. Instinctively, I took on the character of a carny pitchman—"Step right up, folks . . ."—that sort of thing. It worked fine for the bazaar. Afterward, I returned to my normal style, but certain colors that I found while doing the pitchman bit remained. The bazaar took me another step further in the development of a style.

At first, you will be more concerned with performing your tricks properly than with such advanced problems as style. But I have included this brief discussion to give you something to think about as you progress.

Direction and Misdirection

When performing a trick, your behavior must be natural and unforced, but all your gestures and speech cannot have the same value. You must stress certain moments and downplay others. This is called direction, guiding your audience's attention toward the important points so they will fully appreciate the climax. Nothing is so disconcerting as to conclude a trick and learn, from the mild response, that you have lost most of the audience along the way.

Misdirection is central to the art of magic. An audience's attention can be diverted in many ways—a glance, a gesture, a turn, a question, a remark. The basic rule of misdirection is to look at a point you wish the audience to watch. If you have a coin palmed in your right hand, your gaze should be directed toward your left hand. Often, by looking directly at the audience you can divert their attention from your hands for a moment or two.

In some ways misdirection is easier for the close-up magician than it is for the stage magician, who is under constant scrutiny. The close-up magician, working informally at the dinner table or in a living room, can turn the intimate quarters to his advantage through personal contact with the spectators and can often disarm them in ways a stage performer could never manage.

When I was in my early teens, I was given a copy of *The Modern Conjuror* by C. Lang Neil, even then a relic of a bygone age but still an excellent first book for a boy. One of the tricks I learned from this book was Charles Bertram's version of the cards up the sleeve, a classic routine in which the magician passes twelve cards from his left hand invisibly into his right pocket.

There comes a point early in this trick when the magician shows his pocket to be empty and immediately afterward palms six cards from the packet of twelve held in his left hand. According to the text, he was supposed to say, "As you can see, my pocket is empty, which is nothing unusual," and then palm the six cards. No explanation for this bit of patter was given, but on performing the trick I discovered that Mr. Bertram was a master of misdirection. When I said, "which is nothing unusual," the audience laughed, and in that split second I was able to palm the cards unobserved.

I have been performing the cards up the sleeve for over thirty years and have never deviated from this bit of misdirection. Every time I say, "which is nothing unusual," the audience laughs, and I palm the cards without a worry. The point here is that even such a small diversion as laughter can distract an audience sufficiently for you to perform an important move.

In explaining the tricks in this book, I have, whenever possible, given tips for misdirection. These may or may not suit your own personality and style. If the method I suggest seems unnatural, you must find your own way. Misdirection grows out of practicing and performing a trick, and you will no doubt evolve many different ways as you continue to work on your magic.

Performing Magic

How do you actually perform magic? Where do you stand or sit? What are the best conditions? How do you begin? How long should you perform? These are legitimate concerns and all affect presentation in some way; hence they are included in this chapter.

There are basically two situations in which you can perform the kind of magic in this book. Real close-up magic—card and coin tricks—must be done at a table. You sit or stand at one end and the spectators group themselves around the other end. The other situation is the stand-up show in a living room. The spectators sit on chairs or sofas at one end of the

room and you stand at the other end. For this kind of show
you need more visual magic—the vanishing silk, the cut and
restored ribbon, the spongeballs, and certain card tricks that
don't require a table, such as the card in the pocket—all
explained in this book.

Of the two kinds of shows, the latter is the more difficult for
the beginner. The stand-up performance, even in a living
room, requires some stage technique. Also, you will feel more
exposed than at a table and may suffer from nervousness. The
table situation is more comfortable and secure. Here you can
chat with your audience informally and establish a friendly
ambience. You have the advantage of being able to use your
lap for certain vanishes, and of course you can perform all the
effects that require a surface on which to deal playing cards.
So if at all possible, head for a table when you start performing magic.

The table at which you perform ought to be covered with a
cloth, to prevent cards and coins from sliding. Many close-up
workers like to use a sponge rubber pad faced with velvet or
felt, called a close-up pad. The surface is perfect for doing
card and coin tricks, and the dark rectangle acts as a frame for
the trick, giving your act a showy look.

How do you get started? This is often one of the biggest
problems confronting the amateur magician. Here you must
use tact and discretion. If it is a social evening, among friends
who have not seen each other for a while, people may wish to
converse and may regard any attempt to perform magic as an
unwanted intrusion. You must wait for the right moment,
when conversation runs down, when the party needs livening
up—only your own intuition can tell you. However, you may
be asked to perform at some time during the evening—
providing the company knows you do magic—so don't jump
the gun. It is always better to be coaxed a little than to im-

pose your performance on the audience. And let them coax you! Once the invitation to perform has been extended, don't be too eager to comply. A few excuses, a reluctant murmur, will only whet the company's appetite. When you do consent, you will begin at a slight advantage, and they will give you their attention willingly. The other possibility is to drop a hint to the host before the gathering, or upon arrival, that you have prepared a little entertainment and would be only too glad to perform, should he or she wish you to. Then leave it up to him or her to find the right moment.

Once you have gained the floor, don't stay on too long. Work up a program that is about twenty to thirty minutes long, no more, and keep the tricks short and snappy. Start off with an attention-getting trick, a quickie, and then move into longer routines, ending with your best effect.

Try to arrange your tricks in some kind of logical sequence, so that one trick grows out of the preceding one. This is not always possible, but bear it in mind when you begin to create a program.

Finally, follow the old vaudevillian's motto: Leave them wanting more.

2/ How to Palm a Coin

Luckily for magicians, people concluded long ago that oxen and goats were just too cumbersome to serve as a medium of exchange and began using bits of precious metals instead. Then, around 700 B.C., the Greeks took to stamping the metals into coins, which were given value by the state, and since then we have had money that jingles.

The first magic book to describe sleight of hand with coins was the *Discouverie of Witchcraft,* by Reginald Scot, which appeared in the seventeenth century. Since coins had already been in use for some 2,300 years when Scot's work was published, we can assume he compiled tricks of ancient vintage.

To this day coin magic is exceedingly popular. Audiences enjoy seeing magicians perform miracles with unprepared, familiar objects. Perhaps it also amuses them to see us vanish, multiply, and transpose the money they work so hard to acquire.

The basic sleight underlying most magic with coins—and other small objects—is called the palm. This is the subterfuge of concealing an object in the hand. There are numerous ways of palming a coin, but they all involve two elements: the physical technique of holding the coin in the hand, and the psychological knack of forgetting that you have the coin concealed there.

Half dollars are the best coins to use for magic. They can be seen at a distance and are actually easier to palm than coins of smaller value. However, if you are a young person whose hands have not reached full growth, you may find quarters easier to handle.

If your skin is naturally moist, you will have no difficulty learning to palm a coin. But if your skin is dry, you will have trouble with some palms and this could lead to early discouragement. Use hand lotion to combat dry skin, or get a small bottle of glycerine from the drugstore and rub a few drops into your palms and between your fingers before practicing or performing. Magic dealers sell a palming paste that serves the same purpose.

The Finger Palm

This is the easiest palm to learn, but practice is required to perform it gracefully and deceptively. The coin is held between the second and third joints of the two middle fingers. The fingers exert a slight pressure on one edge that holds the other edge against the flesh just behind the third joints (Figure 1). The forefinger is slightly extended, the fourth finger slightly curled. If you hold a coin in the finger palm, you will notice that the most natural position for the hand is a pointing gesture, as shown in Figure 2. This gesture arises naturally in most coin tricks, for if you have palmed a coin in the right hand, it is to your advantage to suggest to the audience that it

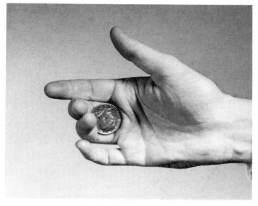

Figure 1

Figure 2

is somewhere else—perhaps in your left hand—and the best way to do this is by pointing.

Another helpful gesture with a coin-palmed hand is to hitch the sleeve. Most spectators suspect the sleeves of being valuable adjuncts of the magician's art. Slightly hitching the sleeve at the elbow, enough to display a bit of forearm, is the easiest way to demonstrate that there's "nothing up my sleeve." (Please don't say it.) Notice how grasping the left sleeve between the right thumb and forefinger and giving it a little inward tug allow the hand to feel more natural with the coin palmed. It will look more natural, too.

It is even possible to show the palm of your hand with a coin concealed in the finger palm and persuade the audience that the hand is really empty. Raise the hand, palm facing the audience, forefinger pointing upward (Figure 3). Notice that the coin remains concealed behind the fingers. Justify the gesture with an appropriate remark. For example, you can say, "Watch!" and hold your hand up to command attention. Or say, "First, I'll . . . ," and extend the forefinger in a

Figure 3

counting gesture. This is not a move that can be repeated often during a performance, but called into play at a strategic moment, it can enhance many coin routines.

Learn to finger palm with both hands. If you are right-handed, all palming will come more easily to you with the right hand, but you should be able to palm with the left when called upon to do so by the requirements of a routine.

The Classic Palm

This is an improvement on the finger palm in one important respect: you can separate your fingers while concealing the coin. No such subtlety as the "Watch!" move is possible

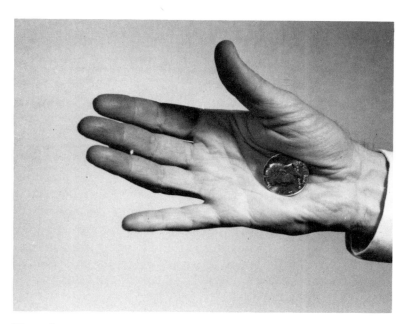

Figure 4

with the classic palm, but most spectators don't realize that it is possible to hold a coin in this position at all, and so they are completely baffled by the consequences of such a conceal-ment.

To learn the classic palm, drop a coin into the upturned palm of your right hand. With the first and second fingers of the left hand, move the coin around in the palm until you find a point somewhere near the heel of the hand where a slight contraction of the thumb and the muscular extension of the fourth finger will grip the coin on each side (Figure 4). Only slight pressure is needed to hold the coin, so don't distort your hand trying to get an iron grip. Here is where dry skin can be a handicap; if you have trouble holding the coin in position, apply a little glycerine or palming paste to the hand and you'll see a marked improvement.

At first your thumb will appear cramped and the fingers will splay outward. As the muscles become adapted and all work in unison, you will find that the coin can be held by the slightest contraction, leaving the fingers and thumb free to work naturally.

Once you have found the right spot and can apply pressure on the coin by contracting the hand muscles, try this: lay the coin on your palm and press it into position with the second and third fingers of the *right* hand. After you have learned this method, turn your hand over, support the coin on the tips of the second and third fingers, and press it into the palm from this position. Finally, try to slide the coin from mid-palm into the classic palm position without the aid of the fingers of either hand. Catch it there by compressing the muscles and turn your hand over.

Again, as in the finger palm, the gesture of pointing or tugging the sleeve, or perhaps rubbing the back of the other hand mysteriously with one finger, contributes to the deception and allays suspicion. However, the classic palm requires practice before gestures and activities with the hand can be accomplished without losing the coin. In practicing this palm, try picking up objects, drinking a glass of water, buttoning your shirt—anything to develop the muscular coordination needed to hold the coin firmly in place.

These two palms are sufficient to enable you to learn several fine coin vanishes and to perform some coin routines. There are more concealments that are useful to know, and I'll cover them here, although you may want to go on and learn some vanishes before returning to them.

Thumb Palms

There are three concealments with the thumb palm available to a magician. Each has its purposes and its limitations.

Take a coin in the left hand and place it in the crotch of the right thumb, the point where the forefinger and thumb form a V, holding it by a slight pressure of the thumb against the edge of the hand. This is one thumb-palm position, shown in Figure 5, and there are two ways of getting the coin there.

The first method is to hold the coin between the first two fingers and the thumb, the back of the hand toward the audience, and to pull it into the crotch by bending the two fingers inward, sliding the coin across the inner surface of the thumb (Figure 6), until it finds its place in the crotch. With practice this can be done in a flash, but the movement of the two fingers must always be covered by a larger movement of the hand.

The second method of getting the coin into the thumb palm is to hold it between the tips of the extended first and second

Figure 5

Figure 6

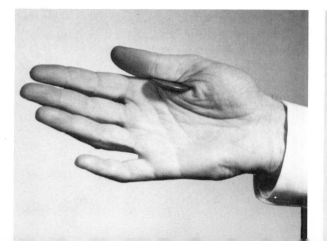

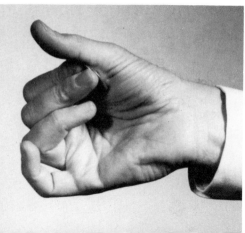

fingers, then bend these fingers into the hand. This brings the coin into the crotch, and the thumb clamps down on it while the fingers return to their extended position.

Another thumb-palm position is called the edge thumb palm, or the Downs palm, after T. Nelson Downs (1867–1938), the great coin manipulator. This is a difficult palm to master and should not be attempted until you are adept at the other palms. When you do master it, though, you will have at your disposal a move of uncommon beauty and deceptiveness.

In this thumb palm the coin is held in the crotch by its edges. To acquaint yourself with the principle, take a coin in the left hand and place it with its edge pressing against the fleshy part at the base of the thumb and first finger. Now close the thumb on the opposite edge and you will find that the coin can be held there by slight pressure. Most wonderful of all, when the hand is turned palm toward the audience, the coin remains invisible, hidden behind the thumb.

There are two difficulties involved in executing the edge palm—getting the coin into position, and holding it there. Both require considerable practice.

To get the coin into position, hold it at the tips of the first and second fingers, at its bottom edge (Figure 7). Whereas for the regular thumb palm the coin is gripped at the inner edge, here it is the bottom edge that must be held, allowing the coin to protrude above the fingers. The first finger is in front, the second behind. Now, when the fingers are bent inward (Figure 8), the coin is automatically turned edgewise and moves directly into the edge-palm position (Figure 9), where it is held by thumb pressure (Figure 10, hand tilted to show coin). After a few hundred repetitions, this move becomes a little less difficult to accomplish and you will be able to try the vanishes with it described in the next chapter. Experienced

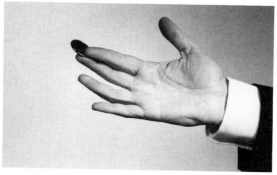

Figure 7

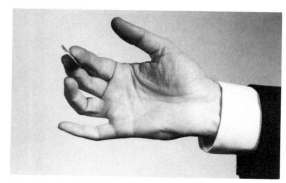

Figure 8

Figure 9

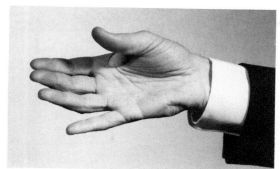

Figure 10

coin manipulators can edge palm a half-dozen coins and produce them one at a time.

A third thumb-palm position is called the rear thumb clip and it, too, has its place in the repertoire of the sleight-of-hand artist. Here the coin is held in the fleshy part of the crotch, but behind the thumb rather than on the inside of the hand (Figure 11, top view). If the hand is shown palm outward and perfectly perpendicular to the floor, the coin may be seen, but tilt the hand slightly backward and the coin disappears from view.

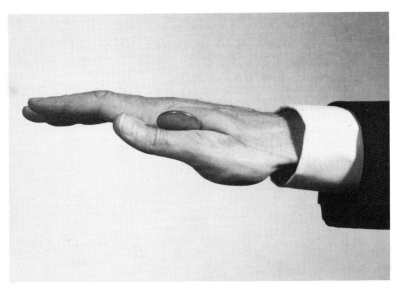

Figure 11

The nicest use for this palm is the production of a coin from nowhere. With the coin held in the thumb clip, hold out both hands as if testing for rain. Look upward. Then move your right hand slightly backward, simultaneously opening your thumb. The coin will slide into your hand. Close your fingers upon it instantly. Then open them—to reveal it lying on the palm. To the audience it appears as if you have made a grab in the air and found a coin. Since the hand is first shown empty, the production is pure magic. If you are performing for spectators of my generation, you can allude to the song "Pennies from Heaven."

3/Coin Vanishes

Most of the methods magicians have invented for vanishing a coin require passing the coin from one hand to the other. Hence these coin vanishes are called passes. In performing a coin pass the magician shows the coin in one hand and pretends to place it in the other hand, actually retaining it, and closes the receiving hand over the nonexistent coin. In a moment he opens the hand and shows it empty. Then, before the audience can guess where the coin might be, he reproduces it from the air or from some part of his body.

The coin pass contains all the ingredients of the art—pretense, belief, misdirection, and suggestion. If you can master a basic coin pass, you are on your way to becoming a magician.

There are dozens of coin passes, but this book contains only a few. The selection is based on two factors—ease of learning and plausibility of performance. By plausibility I mean the naturalness of the gesture itself, whether you would convince an audience that you have really transferred a coin from one hand to the other. Some passes involve movements that are so unnatural that they arouse an audience's suspicions before the vanish is accomplished.

In learning these vanishes, first get the feel of actually

transferring the coin in the manner described in Chapter 2. Watch yourself in the mirror. Then, while retaining the coin, try to emulate that behavior.

Remember what was said in the first chapter about belief. Try to imagine the coin in the hand. The success of every coin vanish depends on your conviction as an actor.

Let's take a simple vanish and explore all the aspects of the sleight.

Turnover Vanish (Finger Palm)

This is perhaps the easiest coin vanish to learn, but it is no less deceptive than some of the more difficult ones. Required are an ability to finger palm naturally and a sense of timing, both of which come with practice.

Start this vanish by displaying a coin on the outstretched fingers of the right hand, being sure the coin lies between the second and third joints of the two middle fingers, in position for the finger palm. Now show the open left hand on a line with the right (Figure 12). Bring the right hand over to the left, turning it inward as it approaches, and pretend to drop the coin into the open left hand (Figure 13). As soon as the right hand covers the left, close the left fingers as if they had received the coin, and slightly bend the two middle fingers of the right hand to prevent the coin from falling. To get the proper timing, practice actually dropping the coin into the left hand.

The right hand does not remain over the left, but continues naturally back toward the body, revealing the closed left hand, and then points toward that hand in a relaxed and casual manner (Figure 14).

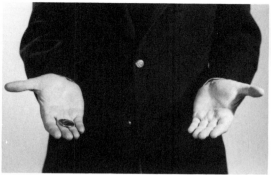

Figure 12

Figure 13

Figure 14

Give the spectators a second to grasp the situation, and then open the left hand with a slight flourish, or perhaps an upward toss, showing that the coin has vanished.

As soon as you have established the disappearance of the coin, the right hand, with the coin palmed, relaxes its pointing gesture and recovers the coin, either from behind the left elbow or from behind the right knee. At first you will find it easier to bring the coin to the fingertips at the right knee, for gravity helps in getting the coin from the finger palm. When recovering from the elbow, the coin must be pushed up with the thumb, while the hand is masked by the elbow. Neither recovery is very difficult, but the elbow recovery needs exact timing so that the coin seems to appear at the fingertips as the

Figure 15

hand comes away from the elbow, apparently pulling the coin from the cloth of the sleeve (Figure 15).

For some reason—and I think I know why—the elbow recovery always puzzles an audience. When the coin vanishes, many people automatically assume it has gone up your sleeve, and when you magically reproduce it from that place—but from the *outside* of the material—you have compounded the illusion. Not only have you vanished a coin, you have caused it to penetrate the fabric.

In presenting this, or any other, coin vanish, remember that the audience does not know in advance *why* you are transferring a coin from one hand to the other. Don't anticipate the vanish by making a big thing of the transfer. Patter is unnecessary, except perhaps to say, "Here's a coin." Don't say something like "I'm going to place this coin in my left hand . . ." Just show the coin, casually perform the fake transfer, and regard the closed left hand with a noncommittal air. Your manner should suggest, "Here's a coin in the left hand. Now what are we going to do with it? Look! It has disappeared! Where can it be? Ah! There it is! Lurking behind my elbow." This is the silent script that you should mime in most vanishes. Of course, when you link several vanishes into a routine with one coin, you start off in this way, but build the vanishes to a climax, generating more and more excitement as the coin keeps vanishing and reappearing in the most mysterious ways.

The (New) French Drop

This venerable sleight is rarely used anymore in its original form, but it once was the first lesson given student magicians. With the important change in the sleight as explained here, it has been renewed and once again ranks with the best of coin vanishes.

To execute this vanish, hold the coin by the edge, between the first two fingers and thumb of the left hand (Figure 16). The surface of the coin faces the ceiling. Tilt the hand forward to show the coin. Bring the right hand over and begin to grasp the coin with the fingers above and the thumb below (Figure 17, rear view), but just as you close on the coin, allow it to fall past your thumb into the finger palm of the left hand. Move the right hand away, to the right, with the fingers together (Figure 18, rear view), as if they held a coin behind them (Figure 19).

Now you have two choices. The first is simply to rub the fingers and thumb of the right hand, as if crumpling the coin,

Figure 16

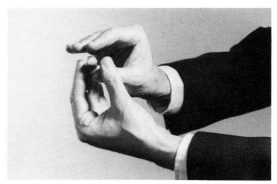

Figure 17

Figure 18

and show that it is gone. The second possibility is to mime allowing the imaginary coin to fall into the palm of the right hand and closing the fingers over it (Figure 20). To do this you must practice with a real coin and get the feeling of the weight falling into your hand. This produces a slight reaction, a dipping movement of the hand, which you must try to capture. Then, after a second or two, you can open the closed right hand and show that the coin has vanished (Figure 21).

Of course, during this time the left hand has finger palmed the coin, turned with its back toward the audience, and assumed a pointing gesture, focusing attention on the closed

Figure 19

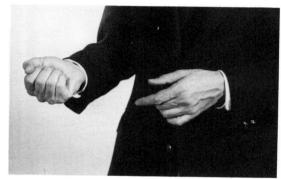

Figure 20

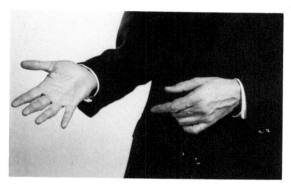

Figure 21

right hand that is supposed to hold the coin. Do not move the left hand after the coin has fallen into the finger palm, except to curl the fingers naturally around it and turn the hand over. This is the difficult part of the move. You must practice getting the coin to fall just where you want it, between the second and third joints of the two middle fingers, so that you will not betray its presence by any unnatural movement when bringing it into the finger palm.

In actuality, it is not necessary to have the coin fall perfectly into the finger palm. If it falls farther forward onto the fingers, it can be balanced on the fingers as the hand points, limp-wristed. The center palm is the danger area, though; from there it is difficult to rescue the coin without giving away the move.

In the old method of doing the French drop, the right hand enveloped the coin and pretended to carry it away in the closed fist. The coin fell past the thumb and into the finger palm. But, as you will see if you try it, this is an unnatural way to transfer a coin from one hand to another. Taking the coin between the fingers is more natural, more graceful, and leads to the clever dip move—a vast improvement over the old method.

The Pivot Vanish

This vanish also depends on the finger palm. It is easy to learn and is also extremely plausible, for the manner of transferring the coin is quite natural.

Hold a coin in the right hand, between the first two fingers and thumb (Figure 22). Bring the right hand across the body, open the left hand at about waist height, and place the coin with its edge against the palm (Figure 23). Now hold it there a second. Push the coin forward a bit and notice how it pivots behind the second and third fingers (Figure 24, rear view). This is the key to the move. As the coin pivots behind the right fingers, close the left fingers into a fist, concealing the movement. Withdraw the left hand, holding the coin behind the fingers of the right hand with the thumb.

Now you must bring the coin into the finger palm without the slightest trace of unnatural movement. One way is to grasp the left sleeve at the elbow, between the first and sec-

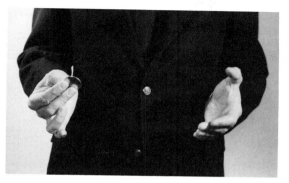

Figure 22

Figure 23

Figure 24

Figure 25

Figure 26

ond fingers of the right hand, and give it a little hitch, bringing the coin into the finger palm as the hand travels toward the sleeve.

Let's go back again to the moment when you placed the coin against the palm of the left hand. In actual performance, of course, you do not hold it there and test the pivot. You push, pivot, and withdraw the left hand a few inches to your left all in one motion—just as if you'd left the coin there. Notice that it is the left hand that moves, to focus the audience's attention on *it* and *away* from the hand retaining the coin. The right hand darts toward the sleeve, gives it a little tug, and, with the coin securely finger palmed, comes back to rest at about waist height, pointing at the left hand (Figure 25).

Hitching the sleeve to cover the smaller movement of finger palming should not be overused. As an alternative, you can turn your left hand over, so the back of the hand is toward the audience. Then turn your body slightly toward the left, move your right hand toward the left, finger palming on the way, and rub the back of the left hand with your forefinger in a mysterious gesture (Figure 26).

Tap-in Vanish

This deceptive vanish is a slight variation on the French drop. The coin is displayed in the left hand between the first two fingers and thumb. Advance the right hand, with the intention of grasping the coin, and bring the palm against its edge, knocking it into the finger palm of the left hand and simultaneously closing the fingers of the right. The closed right hand moves away, to the right, ostensibly holding the coin, and the left points suggestively toward it.

The secret of this pass is to relax the hold of the left thumb and fingers on the coin as its edge comes into contact with the right palm. The momentum of the right hand is sufficient to tap the coin into the left finger palm.

Turnover Vanishes (Classic Palm)

In linking several vanishes, it is advisable to alternate the finger palm with the classic palm. This way the audience sees the hand that conceals the coin in different positions.

The first vanish begins with the coin lying on the fingers of the right hand (Figure 27). Bring the left hand over and, with the tips of the fingers, slide the coin from the fingers along the palm of the right hand. Pretend to slide the coin off the palm of the hand (Figure 28). It's as if the coin were near the edge of a table and your fingernails were too short to pick it up; you would slide it off. As the coin passes the classic-palm position, the left fingers press it into place and continue on their way, forming a fist and turning over, with the back of the hand toward the floor. It's just as if you whisked the coin off your right hand into your left fist. Except that you don't— you leave the coin in the classic palm of the right hand, which turns simultaneously to hide the coin, its back toward the audience (Figure 29).

Now we are back to that important moment between the retention of the coin and the revelation of its disappearance. With the coin classic palmed you can do more than just point. You can wiggle your open fingers over the left fist in a magical gesture, an "abracadabra" movement. Then "dissolve" the coin, perhaps opening the left hand finger by finger, starting with the pinky, one finger trailing the next (Figure 30).

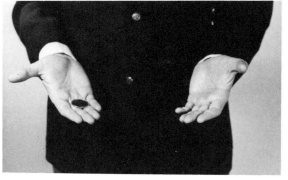

Figure 27

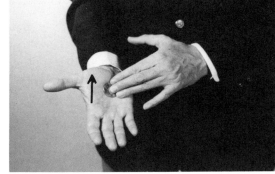

Figure 28

Figure 29

Figure 30

There is a very pretty recovery after this vanish. Instead of producing the coin from the elbow or knee, you open the left hand, show that the coin has gone, and immediately pass the right hand over the open left hand, in a repetition of the passes you made over the closed fist. Relax the muscles of the right hand and allow the coin to fall into the left palm, instantly closing the hand and turning it over. Follow this move by rubbing the back of that hand with the right forefinger. All the moves blend into one action—the right hand drops its coin, the left closes and turns, the right forefinger rubs the back of the hand. Then the left hand turns over again and the fingers are opened to reveal—*the coin!* It's a beautiful sleight, not terribly difficult to master, and worth the practice. I can't think of any coin vanish and recovery that has so often drawn gasps of astonishment and delight. The wiggling open fingers convince the spectators that the coin could not possibly be in the right hand, and its disappearance and sudden reappearance are completely baffling.

The second vanish with the classic palm is a little harder to master; it requires grasping the coin in position without the aid of finger pressure. In every other respect it is similar to the turnover vanish with the finger palm.

Display the coin on the outstretched palm of the right hand, but as you do, jiggle it into the exact spot where you can grasp it by merely contracting the muscles. After a while you'll learn where that spot is. Then, holding the left hand open, palm up, bring the right hand across and pretend to dump the coin into the left hand. Instead, contract the muscles of the right hand and hold the coin in the classic palm, at the same time closing the fingers of the left hand as if it held the coin. Then proceed to show that the coin has vanished, and reproduce it as you please.

Finally, the classic palm can be used to vanish a coin without the usual fake transfer. Holding the coin between the right forefinger and thumb, turn slightly to the right and pretend to toss the coin into the air. As the hand comes down, the thumb slides the coin off the forefinger and onto the second and third fingers, then releases its pressure so the two fingers can press the coin into the classic palm. The hand ends up above shoulder level, fingers spread wide apart. Your eyes travel upward, following the flight of the invisible coin.

Figure 31

Thumb Palm Vanish

If you read other books on magic you will find descriptions of a coin vanish using the thumb palm. The orthodox manner of passing a coin with the thumb palm is to bring the hand across the body, thumb palming it on the way and closing the other hand on the empty fingers. My experience with this method is that either the movement of drawing the coin into the hand is seen, or one has to pass the coin with such rapidity that the trick is spoiled. In my opinion, the only proper way to vanish a coin with the thumb palm is to pretend to *throw* it into the opposite hand.

Stand with your right side to the audience and hold the coin between the right thumb and first two fingers. The tips of the two fingers ought to be well up toward the middle of the coin. Hold the left hand below, ready for the toss (Figure 31, rear view). Now toss the coin into the left hand, closing that hand as the coin hits.

Open the hand, pick up the coin, and get ready for another throw. This time, though, as the right hand comes down,

Figure 32

thumb palm the coin (Figure 32, rear view) and close the left hand with a small slap. This sound simulates the sound of the coin hitting the hand. It's a good illusion. And the thumb palm is covered by the throw. The spectators have been conditioned by the first throw to associate the movement of the right hand with the flight of the coin through the air and its arrival in the left hand. When you do this again, they believe they see the same thing, only the coin remains in your right hand. By now, you can take it from here.

Vanishes with the Edge Thumb Palm

Until now, all the vanishes described, except one, have been passes in which the coin is apparently transferred from one hand to the other. The exception, the toss with the classic palm, while effective, does not permit the hand to be shown empty after the vanish. The beauty of the edge palm vanish is that the audience can see directly into the palm of the hand without glimpsing the concealed coin.

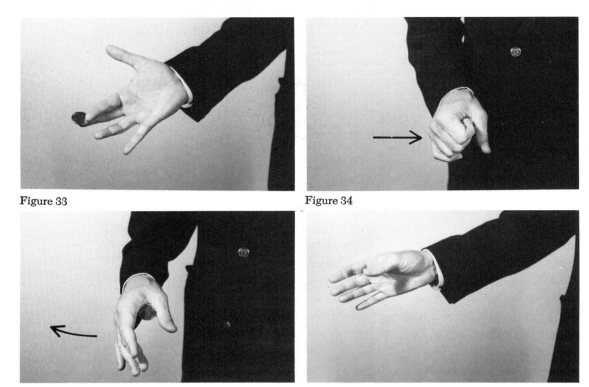

Figure 33

Figure 34

Figure 35

Figure 36

Hold the coin between the tips of the first two fingers of the right hand with the arm extended to the right (Figure 33). Then bring the hand across the body, as you would in throwing a frisbee, edge palming it in the thumb crotch during the backswing, and pretend to toss the coin off to your right (Figures 34, 35, top views, and 36). Don't make the toss too brisk or you'll lose the coin. Just bring the arm gently and smoothly across the body, and not too far to the left, starting the thumb palm on the backswing and completing it by the time the hand pauses. The palm itself is masked by the swing of the arm, and the audience sees only an empty hand at the end of the throw. You have to watch your angle here, tilting the hand slightly downward to bring the thumb in direct line with the eyes of seated spectators. Otherwise they'll see the coin under your thumb.

The vanish completed, pause a moment to gaze above you and then pluck the coin gracefully from the air, recovering it from the edge thumb palm just as you got it there, with the first two fingers. But when it is at the fingertips, withdraw the forefinger and grasp the edge between the second finger and thumb. The illusion is that you vanished a coin and then snatched it from the air with your second finger and thumb.

As an alternative, try this recovery: reach into the air and with the first finger and thumb grasp an invisible coin. Gaze at it for a moment, then bring the right hand across the body, keeping the thumb and finger pressed together at their tips (to conceal the coin), and deposit the invisible coin in the left hand. To do this, pretend the coin is a small speck that you are tossing into the left hand (Figure 37, rear view), which closes upon it immediately. At the end of the toss, a movement of no more than 2 inches, open the thumb and first

Figure 37

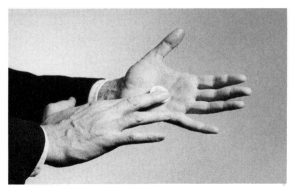

Figure 38

Figure 39

finger, and as you do, let the coin fall out of the edge palm into the left hand and close the hand. Then open the hand and show the coin, now materialized into glittering reality.

It is possible to do a pass with the edge palm, and it is of interest because it permits you to show the right hand empty after the fake transfer.

Stand with your right side slightly toward the audience and display the coin between the right first and second fingers, with the hand held to one side. Bring the right hand across the body and place the coin on the palm of the left hand (Figure 38), closing that hand as the coin touches the palm. As the hand closes, it also turns over, masking the fingers of the right hand, which at that moment bring the coin into the edge thumb palm (Figure 39, rear view). The right hand, with the coin edge palmed, comes under the left, then moves up to rub the back of the left hand—once or twice—with the forefinger (Figure 40, rear view). The left hand turns over again and opens, showing the coin has vanished.

As soon as the vanish has registered on the audience, join the right thumb and second fingertip, thus concealing the coin, and reach to the right, opening the thumb and second

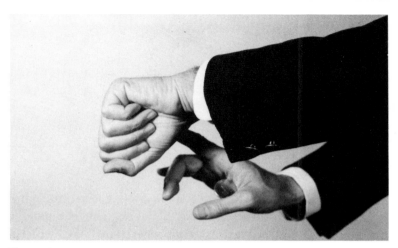

Figure 40

finger as soon as the arm is to the side. Mime grasping for a coin in the air, and then produce it.

"Ping" Vanish

This is a vanish of two coins that I have given the name "ping" because of the sound it makes. I once saw a magician do this vanish at a gathering, but I was across the room and never got a chance to meet him. I went home and tried the vanish and was so delighted with it that I have used it ever since.

Show two half dollars in the right hand. Bring one to the tips of the fingers, holding it by the edge, and toss it into the palm of the left hand (Figure 41), which closes on it. To start,

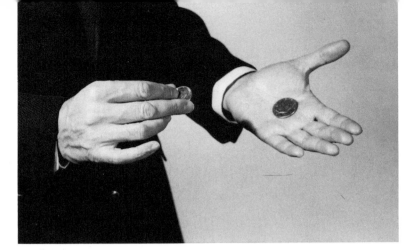

Figure 41

the palm is held flat, with the fingers spread, and the coin is thrown from a distance of about 6 inches. The left hand is tilted slightly toward you; it should not be parallel with the floor.

Now bring the second coin to the fingertips, also holding it by the edge, open the left hand, and throw the coin into the left palm so it lands directly on top of the first coin. At the same time, give the left hand a slight upward jerk. Throw the coin hard. If done right, both coins should bounce off the left hand and into the right hand. The left hand closes, apparently holding the coins. The right curls around the coins (Figure 42, rear view)—you can't get a good finger palm—and drops to the side. The left opens and shows that the coins have vanished. The right reaches down, jingles the coins behind the right knee, and produces them.

Sleeving

No discussion of coin vanishes would be complete without mention of sleeving, the technique of vanishing a coin just the

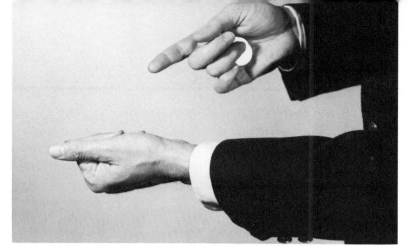

Figure 42

way most people suspect you of doing it—up your sleeve.

Needless to say, the one requirement for sleeving a coin is a jacket with barrel sleeves, and in these days of casual dress you may be called on to perform in a sport shirt. That's why I'm not partial to sleeving and use it sparingly, if at all. It is a good "out" to have at your command, though, to fool the smart ones who suspect the coin of always being in the other hand.

First, sleeving a coin held in the closed fist: this is a quick vanish that offers a change of pace during a series of coin passes. Show the coin in the palm-up right hand; then close the hand and turn it over. Open the fingers very slightly, allowing the coin to rest on the balls of the two middle fingers. This leaves a space between your fingertips and your palm, and it need be sufficient only to allow passage of the coin.

When you want to sleeve the coin, thrust the fist forward; the coin, obeying the law of inertia, will remain at rest—to be caught by the advancing sleeve. Thus, you do not shoot the coin up the sleeve but encase the coin by the advancing sleeve.

To recover the coin, lower your hand and catch it in the cupped fingers.

A more deceptive way to sleeve a coin is from the classic palm. Suppose you are performing a pass which leaves the coin classic palmed in the right hand. You are displaying your closed left hand, which is supposed to contain the coin. Suddenly thrust your right hand toward the nearest spectator, relaxing your grip on the coin so the advancing sleeve catches it. Then turn over the hand and say, "Some people think I keep the coin in this hand, but you see it's not here." Then open the left hand and show that the coin has vanished. "It's not here either."

4 / Coin Switches and Productions

Switching Coins

An effective conclusion to a routine of coin vanishes is to transform the coin you are using into another one, either of a different denomination or of a different nationality. This is done by tossing the coin from one hand to the other. When the receiving hand opens, the coin has changed.

Suppose you are working with a half dollar. Have a quarter in your right pocket and casually place the hand in the pocket and finger palm the coin.

Turn slightly to the left and hold the half dollar between the first two fingers and thumb of the right hand (Figure 43, rear view). Toss the half dollar into the left hand and close the fingers on it. Do this once or twice. On the next throw, release the quarter from the finger palm and allow *it* to fall into the hand.

Now follow carefully. As the right hand releases the quarter from the finger palm, the second finger relaxes its hold on the half dollar and the forefinger and thumb flex inward, pulling the coin behind the extended second, third, and fourth fingers (Figure 44, rear view). The right hand

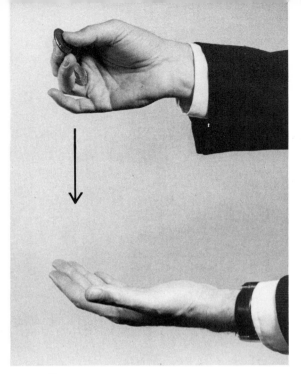

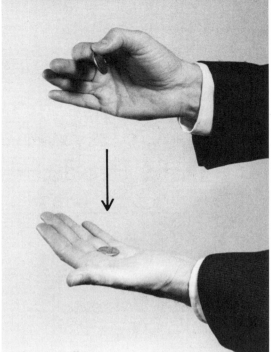

Figure 43   Figure 44

does not stop above the left hand after the quarter is released but follows through, the hand dropping of its own weight to the side of the body. On the way down, the thumb and finger release their hold on the half dollar and it drops into the finger palm (Figure 45, rear view).

The key to this switch is the follow-through. If you don't follow through, the slight finger movement required to bring the coin into the finger palm will be seen and give away the switch. The follow-through masks the move. But don't do it as if you were trying to get your hand down there. The hand drops of its own weight, almost limply, to the side.

In closing the left fingers over the quarter, allow a flash of silver to be seen, convincing the spectators that indeed you do have a coin in that hand. Then give the quarter a couple of squeezes and open the hand, saying, "Seems to have shrunk. I guess I squeezed too hard."

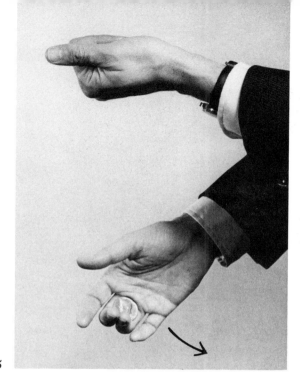

Figure 45

The Utility Move

This is a valuable sleight which enables you to show three coins while keeping a fourth palmed, leading the audience to believe that both hands are empty. The sleight can also be done with small balls.

The three coins are in the left hand, the fourth coin finger palmed in the right. Display the three on the outstretched left hand, but as you do, jiggle one of the coins into the finger-palm position, or push it into place with the right forefinger (Figure 46). Bring the left hand over and drop the coins into the right hand, which opens to receive them, but allow only two of them to fall, retaining one in the finger

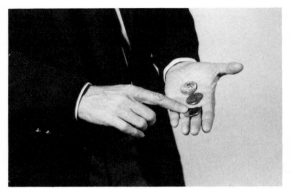

Figure 46

Figure 47

palm (Figure 47, side view). The left hand must come immediately above the right, masking the coin in the right hand, and then move away, revealing three coins. To the audience it appears as if you merely transferred three coins from one hand to the other. Now you have a fourth coin finger palmed in the *left* hand and both hands have apparently been shown.

If you wish, and if the routine calls for it, you can reverse the moves, dropping two coins into the left hand, retaining one in the right, and again show three coins in the left hand.

The utility move can be used with only two coins, if one is a fake of some kind and you wish to switch it for a real coin. For example, magic dealers sell a coin that is an English penny (copper) on one side and a half dollar on the other. At the conclusion of a trick with this coin, you'll want to pass out a normal half dollar for examination and that's where the utility move comes in.

With two coins it's just a matter of finger palming one and showing the other, then turning over both hands as the hand with the fake coin pretends to drop it into the other.

Suppose you have a fake coin, silver side up, in your right

hand and a half dollar finger palmed in your left. Get the fake into position for the finger palm, and bring your right hand across the body toward the left, which turns palm up at the last moment to receive the coin. You finger palm the fake, however, and when the right hand moves past the left, after apparently dropping the coin, the audience sees the half dollar lying on the palm of the left hand. They think it's the coin you just dropped there. Hand it to someone to examine, meanwhile pocketing the fake.

Silk and Coin Sleights

Magic ought to be appealing to the eye. Strive for grace in your movements. Use props that are pretty—colorful balls, cards, silks—whenever possible.

Here are a few ways to inject a bit of color into coin magic with a silk handkerchief. Silks for magic can be obtained from dealers in sizes from 12 to 36 inches square. These silks are especially lightweight and compress easily into a small space. For the following sleights, however, a man's colorful silk handkerchief, of heavier fabric, is perfectly adequate.

1. To produce a coin from a silk, have the silk in your left pocket and the coin in your right. Place both hands in your pockets, as if searching for something, and withdraw the silk and finger palm the coin. Hold the silk by the corner and give it a shake. Then transfer it to the right hand, and give it another couple of shakes, holding the hand with the palm to the front, the two middle fingers curled over the coin, as in Figure 48 (an adaptation of the "Watch!" move). At the same time, show the left hand empty.

Figure 48

Figure 49

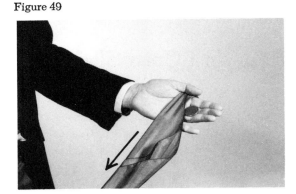

Figure 50

Now turn the left hand palm up and bring the silk which is just below the right thumb and finger into the left thumb crotch, closing the left hand and drawing the silk through it. Pull the silk free and begin a second draw, but as the right hand passes over the left, drop the coin into the left palm, covering it immediately with the silk. Draw the silk through the hand a second time (Figure 49), and just before the silk leaves the hand, swing the left hand to the left, and open the left fingers. As the silk clears the hand, the audience sees the coin lying on the palm, truly a magical appearance (Figure 50).

Figure 51

Figure 52

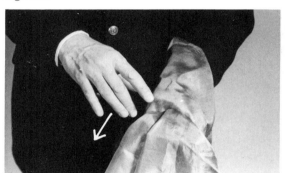

Figure 53

Figure 54

2. The second way to produce the coin begins as in the first method, with the coin finger palmed in the right hand and the silk held in the left. Transfer the silk to the right hand, showing the left empty, and spread the silk over the left palm in such a way that one corner lies on the forearm (Figure 51). Release that corner and press the right forefinger into the palm of the left hand, as if indicating a spot. Then close the left fingers, forming a fist with part of the silk inside.

Regrasp the corner of the silk lying on the left forearm, and ask a spectator to hold the opposite corner. To indicate what you mean, release your hold on the upper corner and reach for the opposite corner, passing your hand over the closed left fist. As the right hand passes above the left, open the left fingers and drop the coin into the hand (Figure 52, side view). The right hand passes just above the left, and the coin does not drop more than an inch, being shielded by the right hand itself. The right hand continues onward (Figure 53), picks up the far corner of the silk, and proffers it to the spectator. Then it returns and again grasps the inner corner on the forearm.

Holding one corner of the silk in your right hand, and with the other corner in the spectator's hand, stare at the closed left fist which contains the center of the handkerchief. Then slowly pull your corner, and the coin will emerge magically from under the fingers of the left hand (Figure 54).

5/ Two Coin Routines

The Gregarious Coins

After you have performed a few coin vanishes as a warm-up, you can then do the two routines explained in this chapter. Of those coin routines that do not require difficult manipulations, these two are among the best.

EFFECT

The magician removes three coins from his pocket and counts them onto his hand. He keeps two in the left hand and puts one in his pocket, but on opening his hand there are still three coins. Once again, he drops two coins into his hand and puts one in his pocket, and again the pocketed coin joins the others in his hand.

PERFORMANCE

Standing or sitting behind a table, remove four half dollars from your right pocket—but don't show how many there are. Keep them cupped in your right hand as you explain that

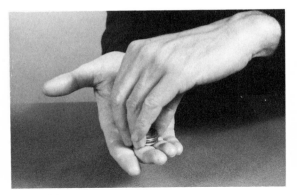

Figure 55

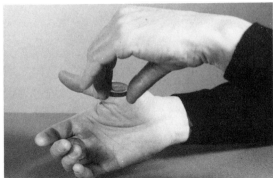

Figure 56

since you hate to spend money, you often keep the same coins in your pocket for many days. The result is that the coins become friendly and gregarious and hate to be separated.

Open your cupped right hand slightly, and gather the coins into the finger-palm position with the fingers of the left hand (Figure 55, side view). Lift off three coins with the left fingers, keeping the bottom coin finger palmed (Figure 56), and turn the right hand inward to conceal the coin in the palm.

Spread the coins onto the palm of the left hand, and show there are three. Move them about with the tip of the right forefinger, getting one into the finger-palm position in preparation for the utility move. Do the move, dropping two coins into the right hand and retaining one in the left. Show the three coins in the right hand (Figure 57).

Close your left hand into a loose fist, thumb up, and place first one, then another coin in the crotch of the thumb (Figure 58), counting, "One coin, two coins in my hand . . . and the third in my pocket." Place the third coin in your right pocket, finger palm it, and withdraw the hand. Now loosen your grip on the two coins in the thumb crotch, and with a

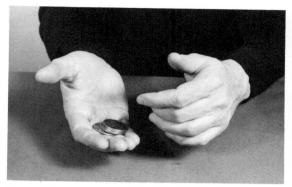
Figure 57

Figure 58

Figure 59

little dip of the hand allow them to slide into the palm, joining the third one already there.

"The coin in my pocket gets lonely," you explain, "and rejoins the two in my hand." Open your left hand and count three coins onto the table (Figure 59).

You have a coin finger palmed in the right hand. Pick up two of the coins on the table with the right hand; display them between the right thumb and forefinger, fanning them slightly, and toss them into your left hand, adding the finger-palmed coin. To do this, just relax the middle fingers holding the palmed coin and all three coins will fall together into your left hand, which closes upon them. Put the third coin (on the table) into your right pocket, finger palm it, and withdraw your right hand.

Continue your patter about the gregariousness of the coins, open your left hand, and count three coins onto the table.

You still have a coin finger palmed in the right hand. This time, with the left hand, pick up two coins and place them into the *right* thumb crotch, closing your hand on the finger-palmed coin, as before. Allow the two coins to sink into the fist, pick up the third coin, with the left hand, and put it in your left pocket, leaving it there. And once again, count three coins onto the table, showing both hands empty.

The Coins Through the Table

This is one of the classics of coin magic, and one of the most bewildering routines in the magical repertoire. When done properly, it leaves an audience totally mystified, without a clue to the secret. Yet the only props needed are three coins and a table.

There are basically two kinds of coins-through-the-table routines. In one, the Chinese version known as the Han Ping Chien trick and its derivatives, the magician holds three coins in one hand and three in the other. Then he passes the three coins in one hand through a table top and into the other hand. The coins all pass together. In the other version, the magician passes the coins one at a time through the table top and into the other hand, or into a glass. The routine given here is the second version, which I prefer because it builds suspense and concludes with a strong climax.

EFFECT

The magician, seated at a table, shows three coins. He proceeds to pass one coin at a time through the table top and into his other hand. The coins pass from the closed left fist, which is slapped onto the table, into the waiting right hand below. When the third coin has passed, he gathers the coins once more in the left hand, places that hand under the table, and passes the coins *up* through the table and into the right hand.

PERFORMANCE

If you are at a dinner table with five or six persons and want to perform a few coin routines, sit at the head of the table and ask the spectators to move toward the other end. They may sit along the sides of the table, but no one ought to be sitting immediately to your left or right.

1. Remove three half dollars from your pocket and count them onto the table, displaying them side by side in a row. (Of course, if you have just finished showing the gregarious coins, you can start with the three coins on the table.) Then pick them up one by one in the right hand and display them in a pile in the finger-palm position, if necessary, using the left fingers to get them there.

Your patter can run as follows: "I'm going to show you an experiment that proves how unstable matter really is. We know it's made up of molecules and atoms, but we don't realize how these particles shift about, and what large spaces exist between them. Here are three coins made of unstable silver and a table top made of unstable wood."

2. Tilt your right hand slightly forward, allowing the coins

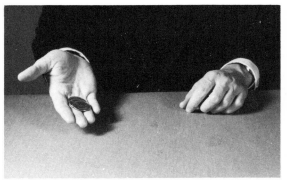

Figure 60

Figure 61

Figure 62

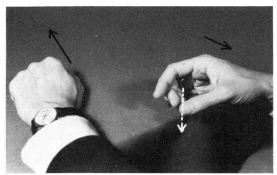

Figure 63

to slide into an overlapping row on the fingers, with the bottom coin still in the finger-palm position (Figure 60). Bring the left hand across the body and pour the coins into the left hand, retaining the bottom coin in the finger palm (Figure 61, rear view). This is easily done, especially if the right hand makes a small sweep across the left. Centrifugal force and a slight pressure of the two middle fingers keep the bottom coin in place. As the coins fall, close the left hand, bring the right hand up in the "Watch!" move (Figure 62), and then lower it to the edge of the table.

3. As the right hand comes to rest at the edge of the table, thrust your left hand, still closed, toward the spectators and say, "Three coins . . . ," relaxing your right fingers and dropping the palmed coin into your lap (Figure 63, rear view). The two moves coincide. The gesture with the left hand provides misdirection for lapping the coin.

4. When the coin has been lapped, continue the sentence, ". . . and a perfectly solid table top." Bring the right hand forward and knock the table with your knuckles. Knock again, and furrow your brow. Raise the right hand, forefinger pointing upward, and allow the audience to see that the hand is empty. Say, "Except for this spot—here," and lower the forefinger to an imaginary spot in the center of the table about 24 inches from your edge. "This is where the spaces between the molecules are exceptionally large."

5. Withdraw the right hand, resting it temporarily on the edge of the table, and place the closed left hand, containing two coins (the audience thinks there are three), over the spot just indicated by the right forefinger. Once again show that your right hand is empty and thrust it beneath the table, leaning forward to reach a point just below the hand. Press your upper arm, above the bicep, against the edge of the table; then bend your elbow, reach back, and pick up the coin in your lap. This movement is covered by your upper arm pressing against the edge. The upper arm must remain perfectly still while the lower arm and wrist bend inward and back to recover the coin. With coin in hand, the right hand returns to its position under the table below the left hand.

6. "Ready? One, two, three!" Raise your left hand slightly from the table and slap it down open, covering the two coins with your palm. Knock the edge of the coin in your right hand against the bottom of the table. Look at the audience for a second; then, with a dramatic air, turn over your left hand

Figure 64

Figure 65

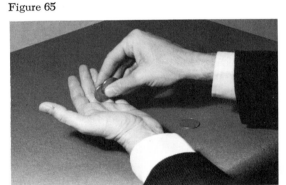

Figure 66

and show two coins. Withdraw your right hand from beneath the table and show the third coin (Figure 64), observing, "One coin has passed through the table."

7. As soon as the penetration has registered on the audience, drop the coin in the right hand onto the table, about 6 inches from the edge nearest you. Pick up the two coins on the table in your right hand, holding them between the second finger and thumb, and fan them so that both are visible (Figure 65, rear view). Announce, "Two more coins to go."

Slide the coins together and bring your right hand over to your left, apparently to deposit the coins in the latter. What you really do is to slide back the coin under your thumb (Figure 66, rear view) and press the coin next to your fingers into the left hand. Close the fingers of the left hand on the single coin, concealing it from the audience, holding the other coin against the fingers with the thumb.

Then bring the right hand down onto the third coin, which is on the table about 6 inches from the edge (Figure 67), and with the tips of the fingers sweep it into your lap. As the coin falls, turn up your right fingers and bring the *coin held there to the tips* (Figure 68). The illusion is perfect. It looks as if you have picked up the coin in a sweeping movement, as one does when his fingernails are short. Say, "One coin has already passed," and thrust your right hand, with the coin, under the table. Lean forward, pick up the lapped coin, as just described, and get ready for the second passage.

8. "Ready? One, two, three!" Slap your left hand onto the table and jingle the two coins in your right hand. Turn over the left hand and show only one coin; withdraw the right hand and drop the two coins onto the table. "Two coins have passed."

9. One coin remains to be passed. When at the conclusion

Figure 67

Figure 68

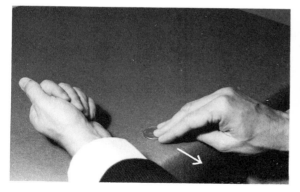

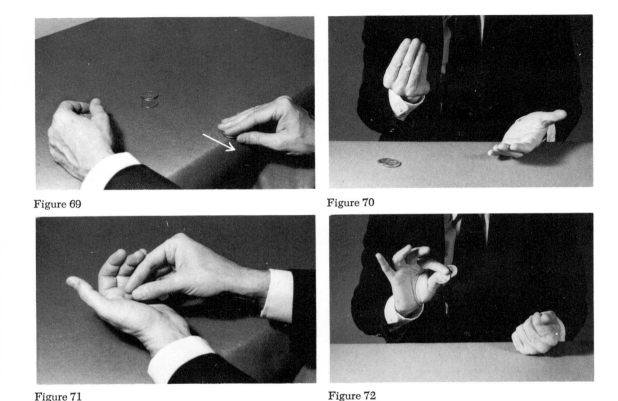

Figure 69

Figure 70

Figure 71

Figure 72

of the last passage you drop the two coins onto the table, make sure they land to the left of the last coin. Announce, "One coin to go," and, with the right fingers, slide the coin toward you, as if picking it up (Figure 69), and right off the table into your lap. Follow through with your right hand, bringing it up with the fingers closed as if they held a coin (Figure 70). Holding the forearm vertically, pause for a second, and then pretend to transfer the "coin" to the left hand (Figure 71), which of course closes. This is a wonderful move, and not hard to perform. To the audience it appears as if you slid a coin off the table and placed it in your left hand. Just believe you have a coin in your right hand; the audience will believe it, too.

Now all you have to do is pick up the two coins on the table in your right hand, being sure that everyone notices that it is empty (Figure 72), and thrust the hand under the table in readiness for the final passage. Lean forward, reach back and pick up the coin in your lap, and you're ready.

10. "Ready? One, two, three!" Once more, slap the left hand on the table, and jingle the three coins in your right hand. Turn over the left hand and withdraw the right, tossing the three coins onto the table. "All three coins have passed through a solid table top!"

11. The last announcement is said with a certain finality, as if the trick were over. Take your bow, seated, and then pick up the three coins in the right hand, holding them in a fan between the first two fingers and thumb. Pretending to place them in the left hand, tap them against the palm of that hand (Figure 73). The coins will slide together, but hold them between the *second* finger and thumb (Figure 74), as the left

Figure 73

Figure 74

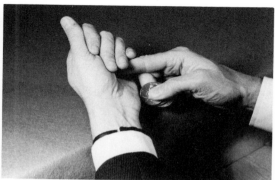

hand closes on the right forefinger. Withdraw the right hand from the closed left, holding the coins invisibly in this position, and rest your right hand naturally on the edge of the table. Your attention is on the left hand, which is over the table, about 12 inches from the edge. Quickly thrust the *left* hand under the table (taking the audience by surprise), and slap it against the underside. At the same time, slap your right hand onto the table, just above the left, turn it over, and reveal the three coins. Smile and say, "This time they passed in the other direction."

6 / Sleights
with Solid Balls

In this chapter we'll explain sleights with solid balls, as opposed to spongeballs, which will be covered in the next chapter. These sleights will enable you to vanish a small ball in several different ways. You can use a rubber ball, about 1½ inches in diameter, from a dime store, or simply roll one out of aluminum foil. Foil balls are light and easy to palm.

Palming a Solid Ball

There are only two practical ways to palm a solid ball. One is with the finger palm, using the two middle fingers to hold the ball lightly against the hand (Figure 75). The other is with the classic palm, using the fleshy extensions of the thumb and little finger to grip the ball (Figure 76). Be sure your hands are slightly moist or treated with glycerine or palming paste. Otherwise you'll find it difficult to classic palm a ball.

As with palming coins, you must learn to palm a solid ball naturally. The hand should look relaxed and unsuspicious. Any of the stratagems described in the coin section—point-

Figure 75   Figure 76

ing, hitching the sleeve, and so on—can be adapted for ball sleights, to help you conceal the ball without giveaway signs.

You have to be careful of the angles between you and your audience when doing magic with solid balls, more so than with other objects. The low angle is the most dangerous. Usually, you'll perform standing while your audience is seated, which puts their eyes on the same plane as your hand, even below it. The slightest turn of the wrist will expose a palmed ball. To compensate for this hazard, tilt your hand slightly—just enough to remove the ball from the spectators' line of vision.

Pick-up Vanish

This vanish and the next one require the ability to classic palm a ball.

Stand with your right side toward the audience and show the ball on the outstretched right hand, the ball lying in the position for classic palming (Figure 77). Bring the left hand

Figure 77

Figure 78

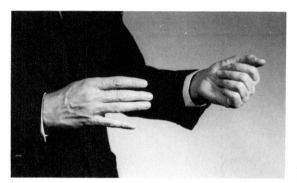

Figure 79

down on the ball from above, fingertips pointing toward the floor, grasp the ball between fingers and thumb, and press it into the right palm (Figure 78). Turn the left hand over, closing it as if it held the ball, and turn the right hand so its back is toward the audience (Figure 79).

The timing must be exact, both hands turning together, the left closing as if it held the ball and the right with the ball palmed in order to conceal it from the audience. The right hand points toward the closed left hand.

Hold this position for a moment, then turn the left hand so its back is toward the audience and rub the back with the tips of the right fingers. Turn the left hand again, give a small

Figure 80

Figure 81

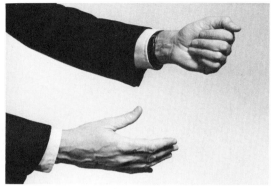

Figure 82

upward toss, and show that the ball has vanished. Recover the ball from the elbow or knee.

Palm-to-Palm Vanish

Stand facing front and show the ball on the right palm. Bring the left palm onto the ball and roll it between the hands, turning the hands to a vertical position (Figure 80). Swing to the left, roll and press the ball into the right palm (Figure 81, rear view), and close the left hand (Figure 82), immediately separating the hands. Turn the left hand, if you wish, and rub the back with the right fingers. Then show that the ball has vanished. Recover from elbow or knee.

Tap-in Vanish

Hold the ball in the left hand between the thumb and first two fingers (Figure 83). Advance the right hand, bringing the palm against the ball, and tap it slightly (Figure 84, top view),

Figure 83

Figure 84

Figure 85

loosening the left-hand grip, and allow the ball to roll into the finger palm of the left hand (Figure 85). Instantly close your right hand and move the hand away as though it contained the ball. The sleight is similar to the tap-in coin vanish.

As always, focus your attention on the closed hand, point with the hand palming the ball, then toss the "ball" into thin air.

Modified Trap Vanish

The trap vanish has long been a standard sleight used by performers of the multiplying balls, but I have never felt comfortable with it in its approved form. Usually, the magician

Figure 86

displays the ball on his closed right fist, which is held with its back toward the audience. He pretends to scoop up the ball with the left hand, but as the hand covers the ball, he opens the right hand and allows the ball to sink into the fist, palming it and at the same time removing his closed left hand as if it held the ball. My objections to the sleight center on the method of displaying the ball and the difficulty of palming it without telltale finger movements. Here is a trap vanish with slight alterations.

Display the ball in the right hand, as shown, palm *toward* the audience, first finger curled to form a small platform (Figure 86). You can stand facing front, or slightly to the right, the right hand just above waist height, the elbow against the body, and the forearm extended.

Swing the right hand forward in a half circle so the back of the hand is toward the audience and the hand and ball are a bit to the left of the center of your body. As the hand moves,

Figure 87

bring the left hand up to meet it and gracefully encircle the ball with the left fingers (Figure 87). As the left hand conceals the ball, the right finger and thumb open, permitting the ball to fall into the finger palm, which is formed by closing the second, third, and fourth fingers as the ball drops. The left hand barely pauses and then moves off to the left, fingers closed around the nonexistent ball; the right hand points toward it to conceal the finger-palmed ball.

The sleight must be performed in a graceful, swinging motion, as a kind of flourish. You'll find that the method of displaying the ball atop the right hand and the movement of the hands across the body conceal the dropping of the ball into the finger palm. Granted, it is not the most natural way to transfer a ball from hand to hand, but it provides a pretty—and mystifying—change of pace for a series of ball vanishes and recoveries.

Mouth Vanish

Here is another way to vary a routine with one ball, and it is a vanish that always delights children. The idea is to pretend to swallow a ball and then reproduce it from under your jacket or elsewhere.

Put the ball between your lips so at least half of its diameter protrudes (Figure 88). Hold it there and make a funny face. (This sleight is all acting.) Now bring up your right hand and pretend to push the ball into your mouth with the palm of your hand (Figure 89), but classic palm it instead. Poke your tongue into your cheek to simulate a ball, and draw the hand across the mouth, brushing the closed lips with the fingertips,

Figure 88

Figure 89

Figure 90

as if tapping the ball completely into the mouth (Figure 90). Then pretend to swallow the ball with great effort, removing the tongue from the cheek as you do. Recover the ball from under your jacket, from your pocket, or from under the chin of a youngster.

7/ Spongeball Magic

If I were allowed to perform only one trick for an audience I wished to impress, I think I would choose a spongeball routine. It is a trick that never fails to amuse, entertain, and mystify. No doubt its appeal is based on the strong element of audience participation that is an intrinsic part of the trick.

Spongeballs for magic are 1½ or 2 inches in diameter, usually red, and very compressible. You can hold one, two, or three sponges in your hand and not know the difference, a fact that, once discovered by magicians, became the wellspring for a fountain of miracles.

In the old days you could buy rubber sponges at the drugstore and cut your own spongeballs. But synthetics have largely taken over in the sponge field, and most plastic sponges don't make good magic balls. Magic dealers sell excellent spongeballs, however, in sets of four, which are smoother than the coarse rubber sponges of yesteryear. These handle very easily, but when two are held as one, compressed at the fingertips, the hand must be kept in motion or the dividing line will be seen.

Palming

Spongeballs are generally finger palmed or thumb palmed. They are too soft to classic palm easily, although it is possible. It is important that the ball be palmed in a position from which it can easily be recovered with the fingers of the same hand, and this is difficult from the classic palm.

The finger palm with a spongeball is similar to that with a coin: the ball is held with the two middle fingers against the pad at their base. As with coins, the hand should appear relaxed and natural.

The thumb palm is easily learned. The ball is held in the thumb crotch by squeezing a small piece of it between the thumb and hand. The ball is gotten into this position by pinching it between the first two fingers and bending them inward, opening the thumb crotch to receive the ball, then closing it and pinching the ball in the thumb palm.

The Pass

There are several passes (vanishes) with spongeballs, but unlike coin passes, these are seldom done in and for themselves. That is, you would not take out a spongeball and do a few passes and leave it at that. The pass is part of a routine with the balls, and for this reason it is not as important to have a variety at your command. The pass with a spongeball

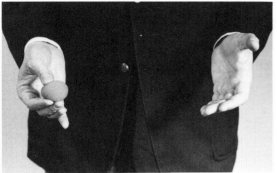

Figure 91

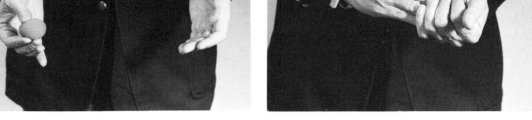

Figure 92

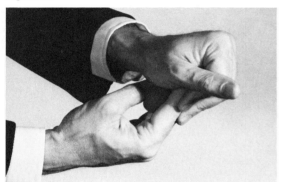

Figure 93

Figure 94

ought to be the most natural transfer you can devise, and so I recommend the following one.

Hold the ball in the right hand, between the thumb and first two fingers (Figure 91). Now start to transfer the ball to the left hand, and as the right hand moves, roll the ball slightly toward the third finger so it is held by the three fingers and thumb. Rather casually, slap the ball gently into the palm of the left hand, closing the fingers on the ball (Figure 92), but don't let go of it. Pull the right hand away, the thumb rolling the ball just a bit inward so it is behind the fingers (Figure 93, top view), and finger palm it (Figure 94,

Open your left hand and show that the ball has
vanished.

The knack here is to place the ball in the left hand with a
little slap. It's as if you were slapping the palm of the left hand
with your right fingers. Do it a few times without the ball.
Just bring the right hand across and give the left palm a little
slap, closing the left fingers on contact. Do it with a ball and
you'll begin to get the idea.

To appreciate the beauty of this vanish, you would have to
have learned all manner of tortured passes with thumb palms
and such before coming upon this one, as I did. The secret of
the pass is nonchalance; you must act as if transferring the ball
to the left hand is unimportant. As you'll see, in the course of
the routine this is quite natural.

The Squeeze Move

In performing with spongeballs, it is essential that you be
able to keep one ball finger palmed or thumb palmed and to
pick up another ball, add the palmed ball, and hold the two
slightly compressed so they appear as one. This is not as easy
as it may sound. There must be absolutely no false finger
movement when picking up the ball, and this is difficult to
avoid when adding the ball from either the thumb palm or the
finger palm. The squeeze move was designed to eliminate this
problem.

The move is very simple. With a ball finger palmed or
thumb palmed—it doesn't matter which—pick up another
ball between the first finger and thumb (Figure 95, side
view), show it, and draw it into the hand, right on top of the
palmed ball, making a fist. Address a spectator. "See how I

Figure 95

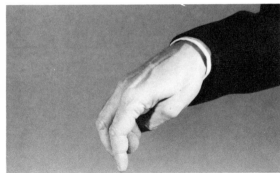

Figure 96

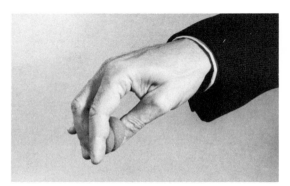

Figure 97

Figure 98

hold this spongeball tightly in my hand? Well, I want you to do the same thing." The balls are held in the fist for just an instant, as a suggestion to the spectator of what you want him to do. At the conclusion of the question, at about the word *hand,* turn the hand back up, press your thumb beneath the bottom spongeball (Figure 96), and bring both to the tips of the first and second fingers (Figure 97). Turn the hand palm up, keeping it in motion, so the crease between the two balls cannot be seen, display the ball(s) (Figure 98), and then place them in the spectator's hand.

The squeeze move is as important to spongeball work as the

pass, and you must perfect it before attempting to perform any routine with the balls. In the routine given here, the move is performed two or three times, but each time the excuse for squeezing the ball(s) is perfectly plausible.

The Final Vanish

At the end of the spongeball routine, there is an amusing bit of byplay. You keep putting one ball in your pocket, but it continues to reappear in your hand with the other two balls. Finally, all the balls vanish at once.

All you need to perform this vanish is a short hair curler, 1½ inches long and 1 inch in diameter, available at any dime store. Get one that matches your skin color. Affix an adhesive bandage across one end and you're all set (Figure 99). This little tube is kept in your right pants or jacket pocket until you need it.

Figure 99

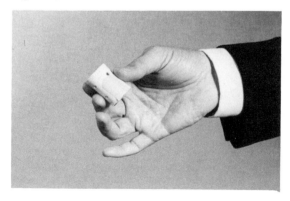

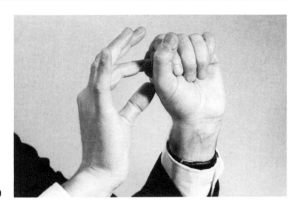

Figure 100

At the conclusion of the routine you will have three balls on the table and the tube finger palmed in the left hand. (I'll explain how you arrive at this point later.) Pick up one ball with the right hand and, turning slightly toward your left, poke it into your left fist (actually into the tube), using the forefinger and second finger alternately (Figure 100, side view). Pick up the second ball and poke it into the tube in the same way. Give it a few final pokes with the second finger, insert the thumb into the fist, and grasp the edge of the tube between the thumb and second finger. Bend the right thumb slightly toward the middle of the hand to conceal it from the audience's view.

Hold the right hand perfectly still, loosen your left-hand hold on the tube, and move the hand back and up, allowing the tube to slip from the fist (Figure 101, side view) and remain clipped between the right thumb and second finger. As the left hand moves to the left, it turns over, still closed, fingers toward the audience (Figure 102, front view). Bend the right second finger inward, concealing the tube, and instantly pick up the third ball (Figure 103, hand tilted to show tube) and thrust it into your right pocket, leaving the tube.

These moves are accompanied by the running patter "One

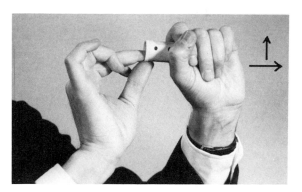

Figure 101

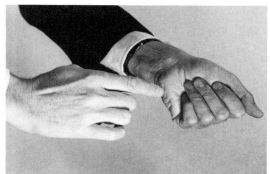

Figure 102

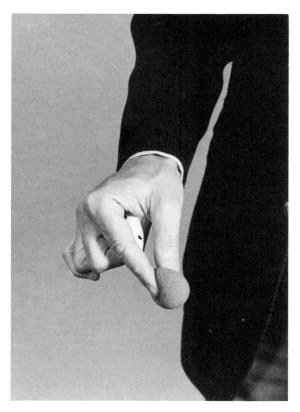

Figure 103

ball in my hand, two balls in my hand, and the third ball in my pocket." Pause a moment and then ask the spectator assisting you, "How many balls in my hand?" Before the assistant can answer, crumple the "balls" in your left hand over his or her hand, showing that they have vanished.

Note that the right hand masks the left when the steal is made, but since the left comes into view instantly, the audience is not aware that it has been obscured. If done properly, the steal is absolutely undetectable, the vanish totally inexplicable.

The conventional method for vanishing the balls at the end of a routine is with a large thumb tip. The balls are poked into the thumb tip, which is concealed in the left fist, like the tube, and the tip withdrawn on the thumb. I consider the tube vanish superior, for it is unnatural to poke a spongeball into your fist with your thumb.

The Routine

The basic theme of every spongeball routine is the passage of a ball from the magician's hand into the hand of a spectator. Every routine uses variations on this theme, but they all have in common the participation of one or more spectators.

EFFECT

The magician takes two spongeballs from his pocket and places one in each hand. He taps his fists on the table and causes the ball in the left hand to vanish and appear in the right hand.

Next the magician places one ball in his left hand and the other ball in the spectator's hand. On command the ball in his hand vanishes and joins the ball in the spectator's hand.

Taking a third ball from his pocket, the magician places two balls in the spectator's hand and one ball in his own. Once again the ball in his hand vanishes and appears in the hand of the spectator.

Finally, after some byplay, all three balls vanish from the magician's hand.

PERFORMANCE

The spongeball routine should be done at a table with the spectators grouped opposite you. Watch out for spectators edging around to the side. However, the spectator who assists you should sit near you, preferably on your left.

To prepare for the routine, place four spongeballs and the tube vanisher (hair curler) in your right pocket.

Reach into your pocket and remove two spongeballs. Roll them onto the table, displaying them freely, but do not pass them for examination. (The spectator who assists you examines them when they are in her or his hand.) Your patter can revolve around the theme of "reproductive cells," alluding to the cellular nature of the balls.

Pick up one spongeball in the right hand, pretend to transfer it to the left hand, but retain it in the right (the pass). Pick up the other ball in the right hand, do the squeeze move, and show both balls at the fingertips, allowing the audience to see that the hand is empty. Then bring both balls into the fist. Tap the knuckles of both fists on the table. Open your left hand with a slight tossing motion toward the right, and then open your right hand and allow the two balls to roll out.

Ask a spectator sitting at your left—preferably of the opposite sex—to hold out her (or his) right hand, and place one of the balls on her open palm. With your right hand, pick up the other ball and do the pass. Then pick up the ball on her hand and say, "Do you see how I hold this spongeball tightly in my hand? Well, I want you to hold this ball the same way." As you draw the balls into your fist, say, "Remember, hold it tightly, like this, so I can't get it away from you." Then bring both balls, compressed as one, to your fingertips, and place them in *her* hand (Figure 104). In doing so, bring your thumb under her fingers to help her close them; then with your thumb on top and fingers beneath her hand, squeeze slightly, repeating, "Tightly, now."

Place your closed left fist against her fist, knuckles against

Figure 104

knuckles, and ask her to press. Exert some pressure yourself.
After a moment, relax the pressure. Point to the crease between her second and third fingers and say, "Do you see that
small opening between your second and third fingers? I have
one, too. Well, my spongeball has left my hand and passed
through that space into yours." Open your hand and show
that the ball has vanished. Tell your assistant to open her
hand, and be prepared for a cry of astonishment.

As the two balls spring from her hand, there will be excla-
mations and remarks from the audience. The spongeballs will
be vigorously examined. During this small commotion, reach
into your pocket, thumb palm (or finger palm) one ball, and
withdraw the other at your fingertips. Toss this ball onto the
table, alongside the other two, and say, "Let's try that again.
This time we'll use another ball."

Pick up one ball in each hand and display them. Say, "Remember how you held the ball in your hand, tightly?" Do the
squeeze move with the ball palmed in your right hand. "Well,
now I want you to hold two balls the same way."

You are now going to place the three balls into your assistant's hand under the pretense of giving her two. Ask her to
hold out her right hand again, palm up, and press the ball in
your left hand and the two compressed balls in your right into
her palm. Slip your thumbs beneath her fingers and use them
to help her close her hand tightly over the balls.

Now pick up the last ball in the right hand and pretend to
transfer it to the left, but do the pass. This time, don't press
your fist against hers; just pretend to throw the ball in your
left hand at her hand, opening your hand and showing that
the ball has vanished. Tell her to open her hand, and watch
her astonishment again when three balls roll out.

You have one ball finger palmed in your right hand. As
soon as the audience settles down, pick up a ball from the

table and slap it into your left hand, adding the palmed ball, and close the hand into a fist, saying, "One ball." Pick up the second ball, poke it into the closed fist, and say, "Two balls." Pick up the third ball and put it in your pocket, saying, "And the third ball in my pocket." Finger palm the ball and withdraw your hand. Turn to your assistant and ask, "How many balls in my hand?" Most likely she'll say two. Open your hand and show three balls.

"Perhaps you weren't watching closely. Let me do that again." Repeat the same routine, putting one ball (and the palmed ball) in the hand, adding the second, and depositing the third in the pocket. This time, however, don't palm the pocketed ball; instead get the tube onto the second finger, bend the finger into the palm, and withdraw your hand. When you open your left hand and again show three balls, letting them roll onto the table, bring both hands together momentarily, extend the right second finger, and press the tube into the left finger palm.

With an air of mock impatience, start the same routine again, but this time tuck the first two balls into the tube, which is now concealed in the left fist. Steal the tube as explained previously (page 80) and whisk the third ball into the pocket, leaving the tube and withdrawing the hand. This time, when you open your hand, the balls have vanished.

Note that the first time you pass the ball into the spectator's hand you press your fist against hers. This prevents her from opening her hand. Also, by actually bringing your hand into contact with hers, you arouse some suspicion that you may *somehow* have maneuvered the ball into her hand, diverting attention from the real secret—that you gave her two balls to begin with. The byplay about the space between the fingers focuses attention on the moment and away from the preceding moment. By the time the spectator has opened her hand, nobody remembers exactly what you did, but everyone will swear you put one ball in your own hand and one in hers.

The second passage is performed without the hand contact to provide a change of pace and further confuse the onlookers. While they are puzzling about the possibility of your squeezing the ball into her hand by contact, you perform the same miracle without even touching her hand.

Practice this routine until you can perform it fluently. I guarantee that it will bewilder any audience.

8/ Simple Card Sleights

If you play any of the popular card games, you probably have suffered through the ordeal of watching a friend perform a card trick or two. It usually goes like this. The would-be magician interrupts the game to announce that he'll show you a "terrific card trick." He clumsily shuffles a badly worn deck, hands you the cards, and asks you to "count the cards into four separate piles." After you have finished this stimulating exercise, your friend says, "Now when I turn my back, look at the top card of any pile, remember it, and then shuffle it back into that pile." Since you are an agreeable and cooperative person, you follow instructions. Your friend then asks you to "point to the pile that contains your card." Again you comply. He picks up the deck and deals four piles of cards onto the table, and asks you again in which pile your card is located. And after a few more deals and counts, he triumphantly discloses your card and beams at you in hope of appreciation.

Now you do not know exactly how, after all this dealing and counting, he managed to find your card; and the truth of the matter is, you don't really care. You are puzzled by this "trick" but you are not mystified—and you have not been entertained. The process that led up to the disclosure of your card was tedious and time-consuming, and the disclosure itself lacked drama. You have seen a card "trick," but you have not seen card "magic."

In fact, few people you'll encounter have seen a capable card magician perform. To judge from the number of books on advanced card magic published annually, there is a sizable population of card magicians, or cardmen, as they are known in magic circles, but the average person may go through life without meeting one.

What distinguishes the card trickster from the cardman? The former merely puzzles; the latter entertains. The card-man entertains because his tricks are little plays that have plots and climaxes, that hold our attention, keep us in suspense, and delight us with a surprise ending.

For example, the trickster will ask to have a card selected and returned to the deck and, as described above, proceed to bore us with an interminable amount of counting and dealing. The cardman can control the card and reveal it instantly, in an amusing manner. He may cut the deck and ask if the cut-to card is the chosen one. No? In a twinkling he changes it—to the chosen card. Cards change, vanish, appear in different parts of the deck, transport themselves from one place to another.

This is the kind of card magic you are going to learn in the following chapters. It does not take great skill, but it does take practice to perform the sleights and routines smoothly and convincingly. If you are already a card player, your feeling for the deck and your familiarity with simple shuffles and cuts will stand you in good stead. If you have not handled cards often, keep a deck handy at home and just play with them while talking, watching TV, or relaxing. Get to know them well.

The cards you use for magic ought to be in good condition. Don't use a dirty, dog-eared deck that has seen duty at the beach. If you are a young person with small hands, perhaps a bridge-size deck (with white borders) will be easier for you to handle than the standard poker deck. Otherwise, the best cards for magic are poker decks with white borders available at any stationery store. Unless cards have white borders, a reversed card can be seen at the edge of the deck. When spanking new, a deck of cards is a little hard to handle, and you'll have to break it in by shuffling and riffling for a while. Then some of the extreme slickness and stiffness wears off and the cards begin to obey your commands a little better.

As a beginner you ought to learn how to accomplish three basic maneuvers. You ought to be able to keep control of a chosen card returned to the deck, bring it to the top or bottom, and shuffle and cut the deck without disturbing the position of the card. This is basic card work, and it is here that we begin.

Overhand Shuffle, True and False

The first maneuver you should learn with a deck of cards is the simple overhand shuffle, which you probably do naturally when it's your turn to deal in a card game. Once you can overhand shuffle smoothly and briskly, you can then false shuffle—that is, pretend to shuffle while actually keeping a card or cards exactly where you want them.

Let's assume the deck is on the table. Pick it up with the right hand, perhaps sliding it off the edge toward you, and drop it into the left, face down, grasping it with the thumb on one side, fingers on the other. Bring the fingers below the face of the deck and lever it into an upright position. Now you

Figure 105

can grasp it in the right hand in the proper manner for shuffling.

Grasp the deck with the second and third fingers at one end, the thumb at the other, and the index finger on the top edge (Figure 105). Some cardmen recommend grasping the deck with the first three fingers at one end, but I find that the index finger on top helps to control the deck. Try it both ways, though, and stick to the one you like best.

The deck is in the right hand, having been lifted from the left. Bring up the left hand, place the thumb on the top edge of the deck, and pull off about half the cards into the left hand, dropping that hand a few inches below the right.

Now the left thumb presses against the back of the half pack in the right hand and pulls down cards, singly and in small packets, letting them drop on the cards already in the left hand (Figure 106), until all the cards have been thumbed off into that hand. Immediately regrasp the deck in the right hand, thumb off half the cards, shuffle them into the left hand singly or in small packets, and repeat once or twice more.

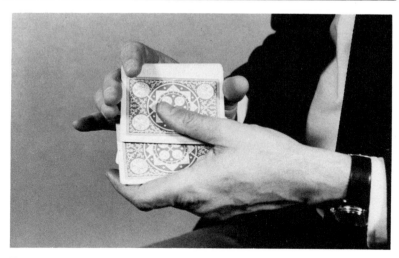

Figure 106

The shuffle should be accomplished with a smooth up and down movement of both hands, meeting and separating as the thumb pulls off cards from the deck.

Practice this shuffle just as described; it is the basis of the *false* overhand shuffle which enables you to keep a card or cards on the top of the deck while the audience believes you are shuffling fairly.

To false shuffle and keep the top card in place, thumb off only the top card into the left hand on the first move; then thumb off a small packet of cards on top of the top card and shuffle off the rest of the cards, singly or in small packets, until you reach the end of the deck. Then shuffle the deck again, thumbing off the cards in small packets until you get near the bottom, when you thumb them off singly, throwing the last card, the original top card, back on top.

In the same way, the bottom card of the deck can be kept in place by shuffling it to the top and then shuffling it back to the bottom.

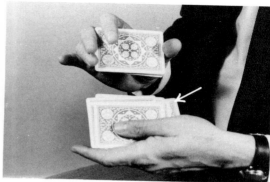

Figure 107   Figure 108

There is a more professional method of false overhand shuffling which keeps not only the top card in place but at least half the deck.

Begin the shuffle by pulling off half the deck with the thumb and letting it fall into the left hand. Bring the thumb up again, press it gently against the top card of the deck, and pull it down, but *bend the thumb inward slightly* so the card slides onto the left-hand packet with its end overhanging the rear of the deck by about a half-inch or more (arrow in Figure 107, side view). This is called an "in-jog" and it's a devilishly clever device for keeping track of a card or cards.

Another method of in-jogging the card is to move the right hand slightly to the rear, so that when the left thumb pulls off the card, it will overhang the rear of the deck.

Shuffle off the rest of the cards onto the in-jogged card (Figure 108), but be sure they are roughly aligned with the packet, so that when you have finished, the in-jogged card will protrude (arrow, Figure 108), locating the card below it.

As soon as all the cards have been shuffled into the left hand, press the right thumb tip against the in-jogged card, breaking the deck at that point (Figure 109, side view). Pick up all the cards below the in-jogged card, thumb on one side,

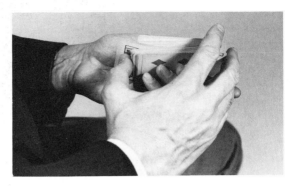

Figure 109

fingers at the other, and drop them on top of the other packet. In other words, cut the deck, bringing the original top card back to the top. To the audience, which, by the way, is directly in front of you and can't see the in-jogged card, it appears as if you shuffled the deck, then tossed one last packet of cards onto the left-hand packet. You've seen card players do this at the end of a shuffle; it looks completely natural.

That's the false overhand shuffle. Practice it until it's second nature. Keep a couple of aces on top of the deck and practice false shuffling continuously, keeping them on top as long as you can.

Riffle Shuffle

Anybody who has played cards has probably used the riffle shuffle to mix the deck. It is the shuffle preferred by most card players, since it appears to be more open and aboveboard than the overhand. The deck is split in half and held in each hand, and the cards are released by the thumbs so that they interlace. Everyone has his own way of riffle shuffling,

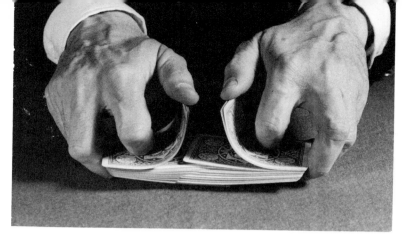

Figure 110

Figure 111

and I'm sure most readers have done it at one time or another. Figures 110 and 111 show two ways to do the riffle shuffle.

The riffle shuffle can be used in card magic to retain two or three cards on the top or bottom of the deck. As such it is inferior to the overhand false shuffle, which allows you to keep quite a number of cards undisturbed on top while giving the impression that you have mixed the deck. But most of the time you need to keep only one or two cards on the top or bottom of the deck, so if you feel more comfortable with the riffle shuffle, by all means use it.

Keeping the top or bottom cards in place during a riffle shuffle is simply a matter of allowing them to fall first (if they are bottom cards) or last (if they are top cards).

The riffle shuffle is usually done on a table; the overhand shuffle can be done anywhere. This is one limitation of the riffle shuffle. Unless you are performing seated at a table, you will naturally tend to use the overhand shuffle or the Hindu shuffle, which follows.

Hindu Shuffle

This is strictly a magician's shuffle that is foreign to the average card player. Although it requires no more dexterity to execute than either the overhand or the riffle, the Hindu shuffle has the look of a flourish about it and as such always gives the audience the impression that you are a skillful card handler.

The Hindu shuffle, like the overhand and the riffle, can be used to retain a card or cards on the top of the deck. It can also be used to force a card, that is, to make a spectator choose a card of your choice. Its prime use as a control shuffle is in bringing several cards chosen by the audience to the top, one at a time, although it appears that each card has been shuffled and lost in the deck.

To perform this shuffle, hold the deck in the left hand almost in dealing position, but with the forefinger at the far end of the deck. Press down on the back of the deck with the pad of the left forefinger so as to tilt the deck and expose the

Figure 112

Figure 113

edges, and pick it up at the inner end between the right thumb and the second and third fingers, the forefinger tip resting on top (Figure 112). Now, with the left thumb and second finger, pull a small packet of cards from the top of the deck. As soon as the packet is clear of the deck, let it fall into the left palm. The thumb is on one side of the packet, the forefinger at the far end, and the other three fingers at the right side.

As soon as you have acquired the move of removing one packet from the top of the deck, you can proceed to slide off packets and allow them to drop, one on top of another, into the left hand (Figure 113), until the cards in the right hand have been almost exhausted. Then throw the last packet on top of the cards in the left hand. That is the Hindu shuffle. In practice it is done rapidly, the two hands working in unison.

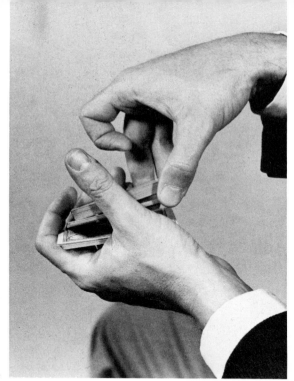

Figure 114

HINDU SHUFFLE CONTROL

You can keep a card or cards on top of the deck with the Hindu shuffle as follows. Begin the shuffle as usual, drawing off about one-third of the deck and allowing it to fall into the left palm. As the two hands come together again, and the large packet in the right hand comes over the small packet in the left, allow the front end of the right-hand packet to rest on the back of the left-hand packet, the front ends flush. This will bring the tips of the right thumb and second finger into contact with the top cards of the left-hand packet. Pick up a small packet of cards with the thumb tip and second finger tip and hold them under the large packet (Figure 114). Continue to draw off small packets from the cards in the right hand, until all have been taken, leaving only the packet that you picked up at the start. Toss this on the deck, thus returning the original top card(s) to the top.

Suppose you want to have three or four cards selected by members of the audience returned to the deck and then revealed one at a time in different ways.

First have the cards selected, then ask the last person who chose a card to return it to the deck. Cut off the top third, as in starting the Hindu shuffle, and request him to place the card on top. Then control it to the top as just described. To the audience, it appears as if you are shuffling the card into the deck. Approach the middle person, draw off the top third again, have him place his card on top (on top of the other chosen card), and again pretend to shuffle it into the deck but control it to the top. In this way, moving from one spectator to the next, you have all the cards returned to the deck and leave the impression that each in turn has been shuffled and lost. In reality they are all on the top, in the order they were chosen.

HINDU SHUFFLE FORCE

This is a very simple and bold method of making a spectator select any card you want him to select. Hindu shuffle the deck a few times, and as you are shuffling, tell the spectator that you want him to call "Stop" at any point. As you finish a shuffle, tilt the deck slightly and catch a glimpse of the bottom card. Then begin to shuffle again, nodding to the spectator as his cue to stop you. When he calls "Stop," simply raise the packet of cards in the right hand, allow him to see the bottom card, and tell him to remember it. You have forced that card! Continue shuffling the deck and eventually reveal the card.

Figure 115

The Little Finger Break

The next thing to learn is a way of controlling a card returned to the deck by the spectator who chose it. Many card tricks—alas, too many—begin with a spectator choosing a card, remembering it, and returning it to the deck. It is at this moment that you must get control of the card. You needn't glimpse it, but you must not let it get lost in the pack, although that's exactly the impression you wish to convey.

Suppose a spectator has chosen a card from a spread on the table, or from the deck spread in your hands. Square up the deck and hold it in your left hand, back up, fingers on one side, thumb on the other. Ask the spectator to return his card to the middle of the deck, and, with the right hand, cut the deck at about midpoint. Grasp the top half lightly, between the thumb at the rear and the second finger at the front, the index finger lightly resting on the back of the top card (Figure 115). This grip is arbitrary; you could just as well lift the cards with three or four fingers, but it gives a certain delicacy to the handling, the feeling you should strive for in all card magic.

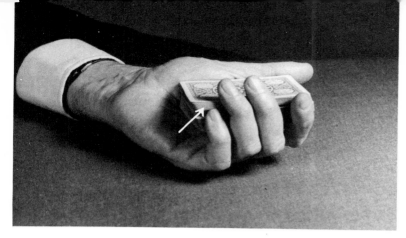

Figure 116

The deck should be handled lightly and delicately, like a fragile object.

At any rate, you have raised half the deck—cut it in the middle—and requested the spectator to replace his card on the bottom portion, which he does. Place the packet held in the right hand on his card, but as you do, insert the very tip of the left little finger between the halves, forming a slight break.

This is the little finger break, one of the cornerstones of card magic. It sounds easy but in actuality needs some practice to perform deceptively. If too much of the little finger is inserted in the deck, the deck will look peculiar and the separation will be visible to the audience. Just insert the fleshy part of the tip, causing only a slight crack in the deck (Figure 116, arrow).

As soon as the right hand has placed its half on top of the cards in the left, it squares the deck at the front and back, running fingers and thumb along the edges, to present a perfectly smooth front edge to the spectators. This takes just a second; the right hand is removed, and the spectators see the deck from the front, perfectly squared, the card to all appearances having been buried in the middle of the deck.

This is the first step in controlling a chosen card. It must be done nonchalantly, arousing no suspicion in the audience.

You should be pattering about one thing or another. Don't emphasize the return of the card to the deck; rather, regard it as an obligatory beginning of the trick that really has little to do with the outcome. In reality, this is where you prepare the way for *everything* that is to follow.

Double Cutting

This is a bold, direct way to bring a card to the top; in all the times I've used it I have never heard a peep of protest. When you first use it you'll expect the audience to guess what you've done, but they won't.

You are holding the deck in the left hand, the chosen card located by the little finger break. Transfer the deck to the right hand, taking it with the two middle fingers at one end and the thumb at the other. The first finger is curled on top. The thumb picks up the break from the little finger and holds the halves separate. As you are facing front, this is not seen.

Bring the left hand under the deck and with the fingertips nip off a small packet of cards below the break. Carry them away in the left hand (Figure 117) and deposit them on the top of the deck, sliding them between the right thumb and second finger (Figure 118). Immediately bring the left hand under the deck again, take the remaining cards below the break, and deposit *them* on top. The chosen card is now on top of the deck.

To the audience it looks as if you merely cut the deck twice. They don't realize that you kept a little finger break above the chosen card, nor that you transferred that break to the right thumb. Follow this double cut with a false overhand

Figure 117

Figure 118

shuffle and nobody will suspect that you could possibly know the whereabouts of the chosen card, let alone have it at your fingertips for instant revelation.

Simplified Two-Handed Pass

The two-handed pass is a sleight that every cardman has spent countless hours perfecting before a mirror. Essentially it is a way of secretly cutting the deck at the little finger break, thereby bringing the selected card to the top (or bottom) of the deck. But no matter how many years you practice the two-handed pass, it is still difficult to get away with 100 percent of the time. Perhaps the audience won't know *what* you did, but they'll know you did *something*, and we would prefer that this suspicion does not enter their minds. Here is a simplified version of the pass that is undetectable.

You have requested the chosen card to be replaced in the deck and have gotten a little finger break above it. You now patter as follows: "Since the card is lost in the deck, it would be very difficult for me to find it. Of course, I could try cutting the deck to find the card by accident, like this." So saying, turn slightly to the left and cut about ten cards from the top of the deck, turn the right hand in a small arc, and reveal the face card. As your right hand turns, the left turns inward and the left index finger points to the face card of the right-hand packet. "Is this your card?" When the spectator says no, return the packet to the top of the deck and grasp another ten or so cards below it, lift off the larger packet, and, in the same way, show the face card of this packet. "Is this?" Again the reply will be negative. And again you replace the packet.

Once again you apparently cut off a packet of cards to show the face card, but this time *you grasp all the cards below the little finger break, with the first three fingers and the thumb, and slip them past the left thumb* (Figure 119), *turning the right hand and the left as before* (Figure 120). Done quickly, it will look no different from the previous cuts, if properly

Figure 119

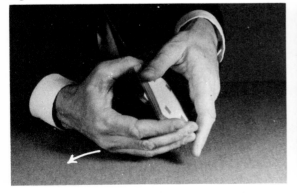

Figure 120

masked by the right hand. But now when you replace the packet in the right hand on top of the packet in the left, the chosen card will be on top. Grasp the entire deck in the right hand, turn it over, and ask about the bottom card. The sleight is done. You have reversed the position of the halves held apart by the little finger and brought the chosen card to the top.

Of course, you cannot always resort to this method of controlling a card to the top. You can use it once or twice during a card act, but that's all. The rest of the time you have to call on other methods.

False Cut

After you have brought a chosen card to the top and false shuffled, it's especially convincing to cut the deck, to give the audience final assurance that the card is hopelessly lost. There are dozens of ways to cut a deck falsely, but for now you need only one.

Let us suppose you have just completed a false shuffle and have tossed the last packet of cards onto the balance of the deck in the left hand. Square up the deck and hold it in dealing position in the left hand. Now regrasp the deck at the ends between the right second and third fingers at one end and the thumb at the other, curling the forefinger on top. The second finger should grip the end just to the right of the center. Release the deck with the left hand and regrasp it in the same way as the right (Figure 121). Immediately cut off the *top half* of the deck with the right hand and drop it on the table (Figure 122). Toss the bottom half into the right hand

Figure 121

Figure 122

Figure 123

Figure 124

(Figure 123), and with the left hand slide the tabled half onto the half in the right hand (Figure 124). There's not a soul in a million who won't swear you cut the deck fairly.

The cut must be done briskly, with a certain rhythm—one, two, three. One, you drop the top half on the table. Two, you toss the half in the left hand into the right hand. Three, you slide the tabled half onto the half in your right hand. The two-handed grip masks the fact that you cut off the *top* half, not the bottom.

The Double Lift

If you have learned the previous sleights, you are getting to
the point where you'll be able to perform a few card miracles.
There are two more, however, that ought to be in your arse-
nal before you start performing. The double lift is one of
them. It is a way of pretending to show the top card of the
deck but really showing the second card. The other sleight,
the glide, is a way of pretending to remove the bottom card of
the deck but really removing the second from the bottom.
Both these sleights are easily learned and are extremely useful.

The secret of the double lift is in the way you handle the
two cards to convince the audience that they are really one
card. Holding the deck in the left hand, square it at each end
with the right fingers and thumb, curling the first finger onto
the top card. As you tap the deck gently back and front,
slightly lift the top two cards with the thumb, bending them
against the tip of the index finger, and insert the tip of the left
little finger under them (Figure 125). You now have a break
below the two top cards. This is done as you toy with the deck
and perhaps patter a bit.

When you want to show the top card(s), insert the tip of the
right forefinger into the break and grasp the two cards, at the
corner, between the finger and thumb (Figure 126). The right
forefinger should be turned slightly, so the top edge contacts
the card. This puts the hand in the right position for the turnover.

Now draw the cards diagonally backward about a half-inch,

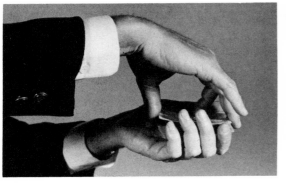

Figure 125

Figure 126

and slide them to the right *across* the back of the deck, until their outside edges contact the left fingers (Figure 127). Using the apex of the fingers and edge of the deck as a kind of pivot point, gently flip the cards to the left and allow them to fall face up across the back of the deck under their own power (Figure 128). They should fall perfectly squared and overlap the rear of the deck about a half-inch. This is how they are displayed, with the request that the audience note the top card of the deck, or with the observation that the top card is such and such. Then, when the card has been duly noted, grasp the inside corner of the two cards once more, push them forward slightly to align them with the top of the deck, and flip them over.

The key to a successful double lift is in the turning of the cards. This must be done casually and lightly; they should describe a lazy arc on top of the deck and remain perfectly squared. Practice is required to give them just the right amount of momentum. The right hand begins to turn the cards, but lets them go and actually follows through across the back of the deck. The movement is fast enough to impart sufficient momentum to the cards so their own weight will carry them over, but not so fast as to lose the effect of the cards

Figure 127

Figure 128

turning slowly over by themselves. This is what convinces the spectators that only one card, the top one, is being turned; they cannot imagine that two cards would remain squared.

This is not the only method of performing the double lift; indeed, magicians continue to devise new and ever more difficult means for performing what is essentially a very simple sleight. One or two of the more advanced lifts are worth learning, but most of them are meant to fool magicians; the average spectator doesn't perceive the difference. Always remember that there are no degrees of deception. You either fool an audience or you don't. If you can fool them the easy way, it is a waste of time and effort to learn a more difficult way to accomplish the same end.

The Glide

As already mentioned, the glide is a sleight that permits you apparently to remove the bottom card of the deck but actually leave it in place. It is useful in many kinds of card tricks.

Hold the deck face up in the left hand between the second joints of the first three fingers and the pad of the thumb. Call attention to the bottom card. Turn the deck face down and curl the second finger inward so its pad contacts the bottom card. Bring the right hand to the deck and extend the second finger under the end, as if about to remove the bottom card, but before the fingertip touches the card, exert pressure with the left second finger and glide the card backward about a half-inch. The right fingertip therefore contacts the *second* card from the bottom (the six of hearts in Figure 129, bottom view) and pulls *it* forward, grasps it with the aid of the thumb, and removes it from the deck. The left little finger contacts the edge of the protruding card and pushes it flush with the deck. Thus, instead of removing the bottom card, as the audi-

Figure 129

ence believes, you have removed the second from the bottom and left the bottom card in place.

There is another way of doing the glide which I think is a little more deceptive. Hold the deck as before, but before turning it face down, grasp it from above with the right fingers and thumb at each end (first finger curled on the bottom card) and with the thumb riffle upward, secretly separating the two bottom cards, and push them forward as one card so they overlap the other end of the deck by about a half-inch. Justify this move by remarking to the audience that everyone can see the card better in this position. Then turn the deck face down, glide the bottom card, and remove the second from the bottom as before. The fact that the audience can see the card protruding from the end of the deck and can see that card openly removed (they think) is more convincing than the first method in which the card is hidden from their view for a moment before removal.

The Mexican Turnover

This is one of the most diabolical sleights ever conceived. It is not a standard sleight that you will use often, but it is capable of producing such miracles that I include it for the delight of anyone who wishes to take the time to learn it. It is not as easy to learn as the glide or the double lift, but it is by no means extremely difficult.

The purpose of the Mexican turnover is to change a card that is face down on the table with one held in your hand, under the pretense of using the card in the hand to flip over the card on the table. The only prerequisite is a cloth or felt cover on the table.

Figure 130

Figure 131

Place a card face down on the table. Hold another card face down in the right hand, at the right inside corner between the forefinger and thumb. Now slide the card in the hand under the card on the table so the two cards overlap as shown in Figure 130. About an inch of the bottom card should protrude at the outer end; half the card at the side.

Now begin to turn the bottom card to the left, raising the top card, and as the cards approach the vertical, slide your thumb from the corner of the bottom card to the corner of the top card and grip that card between the *thumb and second finger* (Figure 131), leaving the first finger to lever the bottom card past the vertical position, whereupon it will fall face up on the table (Figure 132). The right hand follows through, carrying away the original tabled card, and the forefinger replaces the second finger so the card is held as at the start.

It looks as if you have merely used one card to flip over the other. Actually, you have switched them during the flip.

If you have difficulty sliding one card under the other, give the tabled card a mild lengthwise bridge by bending it between thumb and fingers so the back is slightly concave. The

Figure 132

card in your hand will then slip easily beneath the raised corner of the tabled card. This bridge can be made openly during a trick, since the audience doesn't suspect the reason for it.

9/ Card Routines

With the foregoing sleights at your command, you are equipped to perform some mystifying and entertaining card routines. Perhaps you already imagine the possibilities. Since none of the sleights requires extreme dexterity, it follows that combining them into routines shouldn't be too difficult.

One of the most basic types of card routines is the selection and discovery of a card. This is such a familiar plot that it has become a cliché. Nevertheless, when done well, a card discovery, or a series of discoveries, can arouse any audience from its after-dinner torpor.

As I suggested at the beginning of the last chapter, the trouble with the card discoveries performed by novices is the interminable dealing and counting required to find the chosen card. A card discovery performed by a cardman is marked by the swift and direct manner in which he finds a card seemingly lost in the deck. Yet even speed and directness aren't enough. The discovery must have punch. If the card is shuffled into the deck, there's no point, for example, in spreading the cards face up on the table and removing the chosen one, or in simply *telling* the spectator the name of the card he chose. The discovery of a card must come as the climax of a small plot, and it must come as a surprise.

"Take a Card..."

This hackneyed phrase has become, in the public's mind, the hallmark of the card trickster's patter. The words evoke an image of a slick fellow in a loud suit aggressively shoving a deck of cards into a spectator's face. I suggest that you avoid this trite beginning and learn other ways of inducing a spectator to draw a card from the deck.

There are several ways to offer the deck to a spectator, but the manner is more important than the method. The cardman should not *command* a spectator to take a card; he should *request* him to do so—and politely. Here is one way of approaching the problem, assuming this is the first card trick: "Next, I'd like to show you an amusing trick with a deck of cards. Bob, would you like to assist me? Good. Please select a card from the deck and remember it."

This approach immediately makes a partner of the spectator, giving him the feeling that he is participating in the trick rather than serving as your dupe. More than in any other branch of magic, you must be careful when doing card tricks to avoid embarrassing a spectator. Most people are deeply afraid of looking foolish in public. Don't play on this fear during a card act, because they will try to embarrass you in turn.

Having gained the spectator's confidence, you must present the cards to him in such a way that he feels he has had a perfectly free choice. You will encounter many a spectator who hesitates to take a card from the middle of the deck, whose hand roams back and forth before settling on a card, and then often chooses the second from the top or bottom. These people are afraid that you may influence their choice, that you are trying to "force" a card on them.

There is one other requirement that ought to be met when offering a card to a spectator. The gesture ought to look good—not mysterious, necessarily, but graceful and professional. You can spoil a trick by offering a card in a clumsy and inept fashion.

RUNNING THE CARDS

This method permits you to hasten the choice of the card so as to speed up the trick. Hold the cards in the left hand, in dealing position, and with the thumb push them off in twos and threes into the right hand, pulling them from underneath with the right fingers, which also support them and allow you to spread your hands slightly. This creates a spread of several inches within which the spectator is invited to choose a card as they go by (Figure 133). Begin running the cards near you; after the first few, extend your arms so the cards run beneath the spectator's hand and ask him to select one. The cards

Figure 133

Figure 134

should be handled lightly so they almost float from hand to hand, and no undue fuss should be made about the selection.

FANNING THE CARDS

Eventually, you'll want to learn how to make pretty fans with cards in order to include a few flourishes in your performances (see Chapter 11). It takes practice to make real card fans, but it's easy to fan a deck for a card selection. Just hold the cards in the left hand, as for dealing, and with the thumb push them off into the crotch of the right thumb and index finger. Form them into a fan, supported from below with the right fingers (Figure 134), and then remove the left hand. This is a pretty way to present a deck of cards to a spectator.

THE TABLE SPREAD

This is another graceful way to present the cards, and it has the added virtue of appearing totally honest, since your hands don't touch the cards during the selection. The spread must be done on a fairly thick tablecloth or close-up pad, to provide friction and keep the cards from slipping.

Hold the deck in the right hand, the thumb at one end and the second, third, and fourth fingers at the other. The tip of the forefinger rests against the left side of the deck. Place the deck on the table to your left, and then sweep your hand to the right in a short arc, spreading the cards (Figure 135). Use the tip of the forefinger to spread them evenly.

If you get an even spread, you can add a little flourish to the card selection with the flipover. Children have been doing this trick for generations. Insert the left fingers under the bottom card and quickly turn the end cards over. This should produce a domino effect, and the whole row of cards

Figure 135

should flip over in a pretty cascade. Hold the right hand at the other end, beside the top card, and scoop them up as they fall.

RIFFLING THE DECK

There are several ways of riffling the deck to have a card chosen. These methods offer the cardman a change of pace when doing several card discoveries, but I prefer the various spreads. Riffles seem less open and honest, although they are meant to be just that.

Hold the deck in the left hand, with the thumb along the side and the first finger curled against the bottom card. Pressure of the second, third, and fourth fingers braces the deck against the heel of the thumb. Now riffle the left outer corner of the deck with the thumb tip, starting from the top (Figure 136). To have a card chosen this way, ask a spectator to say "Stop" while you riffle. Stop on his command, cut the deck, and offer him the top card of the left-hand packet or show him

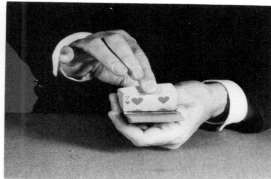

Figure 136

Figure 137

the face card of the right-hand packet (keeping its back toward you).

Another riffle selection can be done by holding the deck in the left hand, at the inner end, with the thumb on top and the fingers curled around the right side. Grasp the ends of the deck between the right thumb and index finger and riffle the outer end with the index finger, starting from the bottom card (Figure 137). Ask a spectator to insert his finger, or a pencil, knife, or pen, anywhere he chooses. Cut the deck at that point and allow him to remove the top card of the left-hand packet or show him the face card of the right-hand packet.

Reversed Card Discovery

This is one of many discoveries that depend for their effect on the magician at first failing in his attempt to find the selected card, then turning defeat into victory by suddenly revealing the card in an original and surprising way. In whatever form it takes, the trick must be properly acted, to persuade the audience that indeed you have failed. Then your success will be that much more impressive.

EFFECT

A spectator selects a card and returns it to the deck. After shuffling and cutting the deck, to convince the audience that the card is lost, the magician turns over the top card and asks the spectator if it is his. On receiving a negative reply, the magician turns the deck and asks if the bottom card is perhaps the one chosen. Again the answer is no. "Well," says the magician, "I'll ask the card to announce itself." He spreads the deck and the spectator's card is seen to be reversed in the center of the spread.

PERFORMANCE

Ask a spectator to select a card, by any of the means previously described, and be sure to remind him to look at the

Figure 138

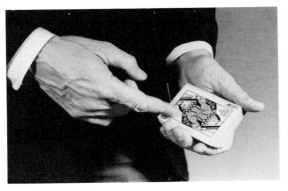

Figure 139

card and remember it. Magicians become so used to this standard opening that they occasionally forget to tell the spectator to look at and *remember* his card.

Cut the deck in the middle and ask the spectator to return the card on the lower left-hand portion. Drop the top portion on top, but hold a little finger break above the card. Double cut it to the top and false shuffle, as previously explained, leaving the card in place, and give the deck a false cut.

Address the spectator. "I wonder whether I can cause your card to appear on the top of the deck." Get a little finger break under the top two cards and do a double lift. "Is this your card?" (Figure 138.) As you ask this question, square the reversed cards with the deck by running the right thumb and second finger back and forth across the inner and outer ends.

When the spectator replies that the face-up card is not his, turn your left hand over and inward, knuckles up, so the bottom card is visible (Figure 139). "Perhaps your card is on the bottom?"

Again the reply will be no. Look disappointed, and in that second of seeming to ponder your next move, wet the tip of your right second finger and pull out the reversed card on the

Figure 140

top (now the bottom) of the deck, turn it over, and replace it under the deck (Figure 140), holding it with the left thumb and fingers, half its length protruding.

Hold the deck in this position and gesture toward the two cards. "You're sure that neither of these cards is the one you chose?" When the spectator reaffirms this fact, push the protruding card square with the deck, using the tip of the right second finger.

This leaves the chosen card reversed second from the top.

Turn the left hand over, bringing the deck back up, and say, "Well, I guess I'll have to ask your card to announce itself," at the same time casually cutting the deck and thus bringing the face-up chosen card to the middle.

"What was the name of your card?" (Suppose it's the five of spades.) Spread the cards face down on the table. There, for all to see, will be the five of spades, the only reversed card in the deck.

The Chameleon Card

Here is another version of the plot in which the magician fails, then succeeds, in finding a chosen card. It is slightly more complex than the foregoing trick but shouldn't give you any trouble if you have mastered the glide.

EFFECT

The magician asks a spectator to choose a card from a spread deck, remember it, and return it. He shuffles the cards and cuts them, convincing proof that the card is lost.

He then tells the spectator that he will try to cut the deck

Figure 141

and find his card. He cuts to three different cards, each time failing to find the chosen card, and places the three wrong cards face down on the table. Asking the spectator to choose one of the three, he then changes that card into the chosen card.

PERFORMANCE

Spread the deck before a spectator and ask him to choose a card. Now ask him to return his card to the deck and then secretly bring it second from the bottom. Here is a practical way of doing this:

Cut the deck and have the spectator return his card to the middle; get a little finger break above it. Double cut it to the top and false shuffle, leaving it there. Shuffle the deck again, but this time press gently on the *top and bottom* cards of the deck with the thumb and fingers of the left hand, and lift all the cards between them with the right hand (Figure 141). The top and bottom cards will remain between the left thumb and fingers. Shuffle off the rest of the deck onto these two cards. When you have finished, the chosen card will of course be second from the bottom. False cut, if you wish, and lay the deck face down on the table.

Address the spectator. "You have chosen a card freely, and

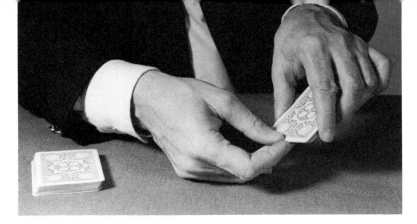

Figure 142

I have shuffled that card into the deck. It would be difficult for me to find that card, but I'm going to attempt it."

Grasp the deck on the table with the left hand in position for cutting. Feel the edges of the cards carefully with thumb and fingers on each side, as if trying to locate the card. Finally, cut about *one-third* of the deck and show the face card. "Is this your card?" When the spectator replies in the negative, look a bit crestfallen. Turn this portion of the deck face down, and remove the card in the same way as when doing the glide, *except don't do the glide* (Figure 142). Remove the card, keeping it face down, and place it on the table. Return the packet in the left hand to the deck.

Repeat the procedure, this time cutting about *half* the deck, failing once more to find the card, and place the second card face down on the table beside the first.

Finally, raise the entire deck and show the bottom card, ask if that one is the spectator's, and when again the reply is no, *do the glide* and leave the bottom card on the face of the deck. Of course, it is the *selected* card that you place face down on the table beside the other two. The spectators believe it to be the indifferent bottom card of the deck.

"I've failed to find the card in three tries," you confess to the audience. "I'm sorry; this rarely happens. But let's see if we can't give this sad story a happy ending."

Ask the spectator to touch two cards. If he chooses his card and another one, push them forward, and pick up the third and return it to the deck. Now ask him to touch one card. If he chooses his card, push it forward and return the other to the deck. If he chooses the other card, pick it up and return it to the deck, and push his card slightly forward. Get the idea? You are forcing his card on him, but he'll never guess it.

If the spectator at first chooses the two odd cards, pick them up and return them to the deck, leaving his card on the table. Either way, you end up with his card on the table. Don't worry about his seeing through this force. In all the years I have done it no one has ever registered the slightest suspicion. Just do it briskly and matter-of-factly.

Then say: "You've chosen one of the three cards. I'm going to change that card into the one you first selected. What was the name of your card? The three of spades?" (Snap your fingers over the card.) "Would you turn over the card, please? The card has changed to the three of spades."

The Magic Number

In this card discovery the magician makes the chosen card appear at any position in the deck determined by the spectator. Again, the trick is one of many versions of the same plot—but the procedure is simple and believable.

EFFECT

A spectator chooses a card at random, remembers it, and returns it to the deck. The magician shuffles the card into the deck, apparently losing it, and cuts the deck once or twice. He then asks the spectator to call out any number, preferably between one and twenty so as not to draw out the trick. The magician then says he'll make the chosen card appear at that number. Counting down to the number, the magician makes good his boast. The chosen card is there.

PERFORMANCE

Have a card chosen and returned to the deck. Get control of it and bring it to the top. Then riffle shuffle the deck and allow the card to fall *second from the top* at the end of the shuffle. Give the deck a false cut.

Hold the deck in the left hand, in dealing position, and ask the spectator who chose the card to think of a number, any number. Then modify that request and say that, in order not to draw out the trick, he should choose a number between one and twenty. Let us say he chooses seven. Inform the audience that you will command the chosen card to appear at that position in the deck—in other words, the seventh card from the top.

Now comes the move that sets up the rest of the trick. You must do two things at once, neither of them very difficult. Thumb off the top card of the deck, grasp it at the upper right corner between the right thumb and forefinger (thumb on top), and in a mock-theatrical gesture, extend the right arm fully to the side, counting "one." At the same time, taking advantage of this misdirection, thumb off the top card of the deck (the chosen one) just enough to permit you to get a little finger break beneath it. Complete the large gesture of counting the first card by bringing it back and placing it face up on top of the deck. As soon as the card is in place, release the grip at the corner and pick up both cards above the break at

Figure 143

Figure 144

Figure 145

the ends between thumb and forefinger, and move them back so they protrude half their length off the inner end of the deck.

Lick the pad of your right thumb and at once slide off the next card, the top one (Figure 143), counting "two," and with a similarly broad gesture reverse *it* on the deck, placing it on top of and squared with the two cards already there. In this way count to one less than the number chosen by the spectator—in this case, six.

As soon as you have placed the sixth card face up on the deck, flush with the packet protruding from the inner end, square the packet with the deck, using the right thumb and second finger. Then thumb off all the *face-up* cards into the right hand, keeping them spread. (The chosen card is now face down on top of the deck.)

Show the fan of face-up cards to the spectator (Figure 144), saying, "You're sure your card isn't among the first six?" When he says no, reply, "Then it has arrived at the number you chose a moment ago, seven. What was the name of your card? The eight of spades?" Using the edge of the fan, flip over the next card (Figure 145) and show that you have succeeded in getting the spectator's card to appear at the chosen number.

The Card Through the Table

This is a card discovery with a smash finish. It is direct and visual in its impact. Best of all, it is not difficult to perform.

EFFECT

The magician allows a spectator to select a card, remember it, and return it to the deck. The magician shuffles the deck, cuts it, then places it in the center of the table. Showing both hands empty, he reaches under the table with one hand and brings his other hand down sharply onto the deck. He withdraws the hand beneath the table to reveal—the chosen card.

PERFORMANCE

You must sit at a table to perform this trick. Have a card selected and bring it to the top. Shuffle overhand, bringing the card to the bottom, and give the deck a false cut. If you wish to bring the card directly to the bottom, that is all right, but if you bring it to the top first you can then give the deck a convincing overhand shuffle and leave the card on the bottom.

Hold the deck in the left hand, in dealing position, but with the thumb along the side, just above the table and a few inches in from the edge of the table. Bring the right hand over and square the deck front and back, tapping it gently with thumb and fingers, and address the spectator who chose the card.

"Will you please point to a spot in the middle of the table. It should be a spot where the wood is a little softer than usual. Can you find a spot like that for me?"

While you are speaking, your hands are not entirely idle. Under the cover of squaring the deck, toying with it as if in readiness for the next step, press the left edge of the deck against the heel of the left thumb, beveling it slightly. This will make it easy to nip the right inside corner of the bottom card with the left little finger, bend it down, and hold a break with the right thumb (Figure 146). The right hand now has control of the deck.

Now comes the important move, which depends entirely on proper misdirection. *When the spectator points to a spot on the table, your left hand moves forward, index finger extended, and points to the same spot; also, your right hand moves back, over the edge of the table, so the deck is suspended above your lap* (Figure 147). As you point to the spot, ask the spectator, "Here?" When he nods, reply, "Yes, it does feel rather soft." And during this byplay, move your thumb back slightly *and allow the bottom card to fall into your lap.* Now your hands reverse themselves. The left hand moves toward your body; the right hand, with the deck, moves to-

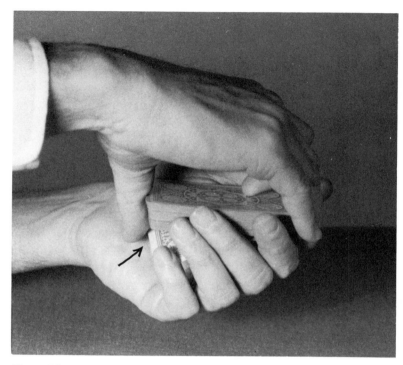

Figure 146

ward the center of the table and places the deck on the imaginary "spot."

You're now ready for the climax. Ask the spectator for the name of his card. "The ace of clubs? All right, watch closely." As you speak, raise your left hand in a gesture that shows it is empty, then drop it into your lap, pick up the card, and extend the hand under the table below the deck. Hit the top of the deck with your right fist, pause for effect, and then slowly remove the chosen card from beneath the table.

As I said, this trick depends on misdirection, the casual and natural movement of the hands in two directions at once.

Figure 147

When the left hand moves forward to point to the spot indicated by the spectator, the right hand moves back *as if in reaction to* the forward movement. It is a perfectly plausible move, and it gets the right hand over the edge of the table without arousing suspicion. Then it is a simple matter to release the card into the lap. Don't allow the right hand to linger too long at the edge of the table, however. The whole business must be performed briskly.

The trick has a terrific impact. The audience can find no possible explanation for this feat. The card is freely chosen, shuffled, and cut into the deck. Without a single false move, you drive it through the table into your other hand. Not just any card, but the chosen one! Try this and you'll be amazed yourself at the response it brings.

An Incredible Coincidence

This is a discovery that puts the Mexican turnover to splendid use. It's one of those tricks that leaves an audience speechless, for you have performed the impossible.

Spread the deck face down on the table and ask a spectator to select any card, remove it from the spread, and look at it.

Gather up the cards and have the card returned to the middle, control it to the top, false shuffle, and false cut.

Once again, spread the deck face down on the table. Pick up the top card, the chosen one, between the right thumb and forefinger, in the position for doing the Mexican turnover, and touch the first card at the extreme left side of the spread with the *corner* of the card held in the hand. (Be sure to keep the card face down.) Ask the spectator to tell you to stop whenever he wishes, and slowly slide the corner of the card across the spread, from left to right. When the spectator says to stop, ask him if he wishes to change his mind, and then remove the card on which the corner is resting by pulling it toward you with the left hand. Turn up the side of the card, as if you were checking its value, and put a slight bridge in it.

Ask the spectator to name the card he first selected. Then perform the Mexican turnover, switching the card in your hand for the card on the table, and show him that he has chosen the same card twice.

The method of having the second card selected by drawing the chosen card across the spread is perfectly natural and justifies the use of that card to flip over the card on the table and thus switch the two. Otherwise, the Mexican turnover is apt to arouse suspicion, since there is no good reason for flipping over a card in this manner.

Routining Card Discoveries

When you have perfected a few of the card discoveries previously explained, you can link them in an entertaining routine. Here is one example of how you can construct such a routine.

Have three cards selected and noted by different spectators, and have them returned one at a time, last one first, bringing them to the top by means of the Hindu shuffle. Give the deck a false overhand shuffle, and at the conclusion, bring the top card second from the bottom by pressing on the top and bottom cards with the left thumb and fingers, lifting the deck free, and dropping it on the two cards.

Perform the chameleon card and reveal the first spectator's card.

At the conclusion of the chameleon card, the other two chosen cards will be on the top of the deck. Spread the deck from left to right and use the top card of the spread, the second chosen card, to perform the incredible coincidence.

Finally, shuffle the last chosen card to the bottom and perform the card through the table.

The Four Ace Trick

If any trick falls into the category of an oldie but goodie it is the venerable four ace routine, of which there are dozens of variations. The plot of most four ace tricks involves the separation of the aces into separate piles or parts of the deck and their ultimate congregation into one pile.

EFFECT

Removing the four aces from the deck, the magician puts them momentarily on top and then asks assistance from a spectator. At the magician's instruction, the spectator places the aces face down on the table and deals three cards onto each ace. The magician asks the spectator to choose a pile and to cover that pile with his hand. The other piles are returned to the deck. The magician riffles the deck and makes a magical pass; the spectator, on lifting his hand, finds that all four aces have gathered into one pile.

PERFORMANCE

Run through the deck and toss the four aces onto the table. Turn the deck face up and run the cards from hand to hand, showing them to the audience. "As you can see, there are no more aces in the deck." This gives you the opportunity to get a break with the left little finger under the three bottom cards of the deck, which of course are on top since the deck is face up.

Figure 148

Gather up the aces in the right hand and hold them fanned, displaying them to the audience. Then close the fan by tapping it against the base of the thumb (Figure 148, arrow). Release the now-squared aces and let them fall on the deck; then pick them up again at the ends between the right thumb and third finger, *also taking the three cards above the break.* Flip the deck back up and swivel the seven cards, which the audience believes to be the four aces, between finger and thumb (Figure 149), drop them on the top of the deck, and drop the deck on the table.

The whole thing is done in an instant. It should look as if you used your thumb as a convenient cushion against which to close the fan of aces, then flipped over the deck and dropped the aces on top. A completely natural move.

You now have on the top of the deck three odd cards and beneath them the four aces.

Ask one of the spectators to assist you and instruct him to stand at your side. Explain to him that you have just placed

Figure 149

the four aces on top of the deck, and, so saying, push off the top four cards into the right hand in a casual manner. Square them up by tapping them against your thumb once more, turn up the packet so the audience can see the bottom card, *which is an ace,* and drop the cards back onto the deck.

Now you tell the spectator that you are tired, having had a hard day at work or school, whichever the case may be, and you would appreciate his taking over and finishing the trick. He'll no doubt smile knowingly and agree.

Hand him the deck and tell him to deal the four aces in a row face down onto the table. Then tell him to deal three cards onto each ace. Guide him so he deals the first three cards (the three aces) onto the last card in the row, the ace. This of course brings the four aces together in one pile. The audience believes they are in four different piles. When he has finished, ask him to place the deck on the table.

You are now going to force the pile of aces just as you did the card in the chameleon card trick. Ask your assistant to touch two piles. If he touches the aces, push them forward, along with the other pile, and drop the two other piles on top of the deck and cut them to the middle. If he fails to touch the ace pile, just drop the two piles he does touch onto the deck and cut them to the middle. This leaves you with two piles, one of which is the aces. Ask him to touch one pile. If he touches the aces, push them forward and cut the other pile back into the deck. If he touches the pile of odd cards, cut it into the deck, leaving the aces on the table.

Now review the situation for the audience so they understand what has happened. Explain that your assistant has placed the four aces on the table, dealt three cards onto each ace, and so on. Point out that he has chosen three piles for return to the deck, leaving one ace with three cards on the table.

Ask the spectator to cover the "ace and its three cards" with his hand. Riffle the deck, recite a magical incantation if you wish, and tell him to remove his hand. Turn over the pile of cards . . . to reveal the four aces!

I have been performing this trick since I was fourteen years old, before every conceivable type of audience, and I cannot remember one time when the response was anything but enthusiastic. The trick can be performed without an assistant— you do the dealing yourself—but the fact that someone else handles the cards seems to add to the effect. The trick is almost self-working, except for the subtle move required to bring the four aces to the top beneath the three odd cards. Practice this move until you can perform it while pattering. It should be done in such an offhand, natural manner that the audience believes the trick has not yet begun.

Four Ace Discovery

This is a quickie that serves as an amusing beginning to the four ace trick. Wait for a time when the audience is momentarily distracted and secretly bring the four aces to the top of the deck. When you have their attention again, false shuffle and false cut the deck, leaving the aces on top. Drop the deck on the table and ask a spectator to cut it into four piles. The aces are on the top of the last pile. Look at the piles critically and cluck your tongue. "Not very even. Will you even them up for me?" The spectator will of course agree, and you then proceed to put him through a series of shifts, all of which have only one purpose: to distribute the aces onto the tops of the four piles.

For example, ask him to take about six cards from the end pile (the ace pile) and put them on the second pile. Then ask him to transfer a couple of cards from the third pile onto the first pile; then two cards from the second pile onto the third pile. (Two aces are now on two adjacent piles.) Ask him to transfer a card from the third pile onto the fourth pile, and one from the second pile onto the first pile. There will now be an ace atop each pile. Tell him he's done a good job and turn over the four top cards. "Well, well, all aces," you exclaim. "How about that!"

If you do this in a disinterested manner, even chatting with another spectator during the transfer of cards, the effect can by quite mystifying. Then go into the four ace routine for a capper.

10 / Palming Cards

To perform magic with coins or balls you must learn how to palm them. The palm, as we have seen, is the basic sleight underlying all magic with these small objects. Not so with cards. I think the previous chapter offers ample proof that it is possible to perform mystifying card magic without palming a card. And so I have set palming apart for the simple reason that this sleight is difficult for the beginner to master and to perform without detection—especially at close quarters. It takes practice to be able to palm cards undetectably, but this shouldn't deter anyone from doing card magic. While you are learning the palm, you can be perfecting your presentation skills by performing all the tricks that don't require palming.

As with other objects, the secret of palming a card is to give the hand concealing the card something to do. The most obvious thing to do is to hold the deck.

Take a card and place it in the palm of your right hand. One corner should contact the pad of the little finger; the diagonally opposite corner should snuggle into the flesh at the base of the thumb. The other three fingers should be curled lightly around the edge of the card (Figure 150). If you look at your hand in a mirror, you will see that it appears stiff and unnatural. But grasp the deck at the ends between the thumb

Figure 150

Figure 151

and first three fingers and the hand assumes a natural air. This grip is the best camouflage for a palmed card (Figure 151). I don't mean to suggest that a magician cannot palm a card and keep it palmed without the crutch of the deck. You should be able to patter, gesture, pick up a deck and set it down, with a card palmed—but this comes in time. At the beginning, try to keep the deck in hand.

Of course, it is also necessary to *get* the card into the palm without detection. There are a number of methods for accomplishing this, each useful for a particular trick or situation, but I'm going to explain only two—the best two, in my opinion. You must also be able to palm several cards, up to ten at first; later you can hold fifteen or twenty. Over twenty is difficult; the thickness of the cards produces an unnatural crook of the thumb.

Palming a Single Card

Hold the deck in the left hand, as for dealing. Grasp the deck with the right hand, the thumb at the inner end and the four fingers at the outer. The tip of the right little finger should be in contact with the right outer corner of the deck. You should be standing with your right side slightly toward the audience.

With the left thumb, slide the top card to the right (Figure 152, side view). The right outer corner should pivot on the pad of the pinky. This will cause the card to slide diagonally

Figure 152

Figure 153

across the top of the deck and align itself with the angle of the right palm. The left fingers, reaching up from below, can now contact the card and press it into the palm (Figure 153).

As soon as the card is firmly in the palm, grip the deck between the thumb and fingers of the right hand, at the ends, and release the left-hand grip.

Palming Several Cards

Hold the deck in the left hand, as for dealing, and get a break with the left little finger below the cards to be palmed. Grasp the deck at the ends between the right thumb and four fingers (Figure 154, side view), and as you do, slip the left third finger into the break and use it to push the cards into the palm, pressing them home with the second finger (Figure 155). Immediately take up the right-hand hold on the deck. This method can also be used to palm one card.

Figure 154

Figure 155

These are the *mechanics* of palming cards, but you must learn the *art* by practice and performance. You must develop the knack of palming a card at just the right moment, and that moment is when you have directed the audience's attention away from your hands. Not even a professional can palm a card in full view of every eye without some little giveaway. But the professional has learned how to distract the spectators at the right moment, catching them off guard just long enough to steal the card.

Card in the Pocket

Among the card tricks requiring palming, this is certainly one of the simplest and best. The misdirection needed to accomplish the palm is built into the trick. Moreover, the hand with the card palmed goes directly to the pocket, removing it from the audience's view, and thus reducing the chance of detection.

EFFECT

The magician asks a spectator to think of a number between one and twenty. Handing him the deck, the magician asks him to count down to the card lying at that number, remember it, and reassemble the pack in the same order. The magician takes the deck and holds it behind his back for a moment, just long enough for him to remove a card, which he places in his pocket. He then asks the spectator for the number he thought of, and on counting down to that number, the card is seen to be missing. The spectator names his card.

The magician removes the card from his pocket. It proves to be the one.

PERFORMANCE

This trick requires effective presentation to achieve maximum effect. If you merely go through the motions, the impact will be lost. You must dramatize the final revelation of the card in such a way that the spectators cannot fail to realize the dimension of the miracle you have performed. It *is* a miracle, in the sense that you have ostensibly read a spectator's mind. So, to get the most out of this trick, you should perform it as an experiment in mind reading.

Ask a spectator to think of a number between one and twenty and to whisper that number to someone else. (This is always a good safeguard.) Hand him the pack and ask him to count down to that number, remember the card, and put the deck back in the same order. Turn your back as he does this.

Retrieve the deck from the spectator and, looking him squarely in the eye, address him as follows: "You have thought of a number between one and twenty and have glimpsed the card that lies at that number. I have no way of knowing what that number is. Please concentrate on the number. Not the card; just the number."

Place the deck behind your back and stare at the spectator for a few seconds, as if trying to receive a telepathic message. While the deck is behind your back do two things: (1) put the bottom card on top; (2) remove the new bottom card and bring it to the front, keeping its back toward the audience. Give the card a mere glance, and slip it into your right coat or pants pocket. Address the spectator again.

"I think I received a very definite message from you. But we won't know until we see the card I put in my pocket.

Nine?" Smile complacently, nod, and count the cards from the top of the deck onto the table. When you reach the ninth (or whatever) card, toss it off the pile toward the spectator, but far enough from him so he has to reach for it. Because you added a card to the top of the deck when you put it behind your back, *the chosen card is now the next card,* that is, the card on top of the deck.

"Will you please look at the ninth card and tell us whether that is the card you remembered a few moments ago."

As the spectator turns over the card on the table, and attention is directed there, palm the top card and take the deck in the right hand, as previously explained.

The spectator will of course say that the card on the table is not his. "I didn't think so," you reply. "You see, I received your telepathic message and removed the ninth card when I put the deck behind my back. That was the card I put in my pocket. What was the name of your card? The jack of clubs?"

Toss the deck into the left hand, thrust your hand into your pocket, and remove the palmed card.

Producing a Fan of Cards

One of the prettiest flourishes in magic is the production of a fan of cards from the air or from some part of the magician's body. Normally a stage effect in which a number of fans are produced in sequence and dropped into a hat, this sleight can be adapted for close-up work, where it serves as an attention-getting introduction to a few card tricks while also establishing the performer's identity as a bona fide magician.

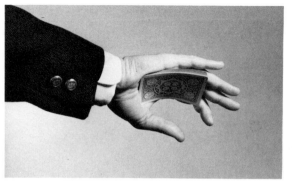

Figure 156   Figure 157

The stage production is usually accomplished by back palming twenty or thirty cards and producing them in fans of about six or eight. This method is quite difficult, requiring years of practice and exceptionally strong fingers. The production for close-up work is done from the standard front palm just explained.

To learn the method of producing the cards, place about eight in your hand, in standard palming position, but with the faces toward the palm. Hold the hand knuckles up, side of thumb toward the imaginary audience. Note that if you turn the back of the hand slightly toward the audience, the cards become invisible. Also, if you relax the grip of the last three fingers and hold the card with only the forefinger and thumb flesh, these fingers can be raised slightly, the hand appearing innocently empty. Figures 156 and 157 show rear and front views of the palm.

Now relax the grip of the forefinger and grip the cards at the sides, toward the end, between the forefinger and little finger (Figure 158, rear view). Bring the thumb onto the face of the cards, grip them between the thumb and first three fingers, and fan them by pushing up with the thumb and down with the fingers, as in Figures 159 and 160.

Figure 158

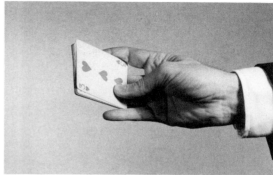

Figure 159

Figure 160

This is the method for producing a fan of cards close up. To weave the flourish into a card routine, either at the beginning of or during your act, hold the deck face up in the left hand, in dealing position, and as you patter, make a pretense of squaring the deck with the right hand while secretly getting a break with the left little finger beneath the top eight or ten cards. (You can take more after you become adept at the sleight.) Now turn the left hand back up and the deck face down for a moment, while still talking, and turn slightly toward your left. When you are ready to palm off the cards, advance the right hand again, turn the deck face up, palm the

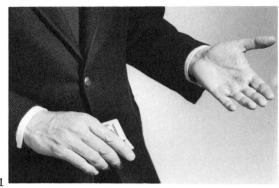

Figure 161

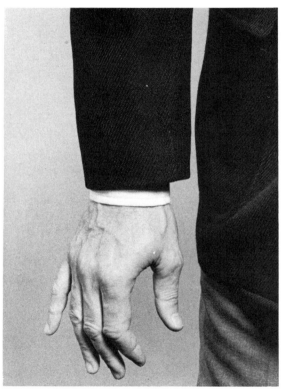

Figure 162

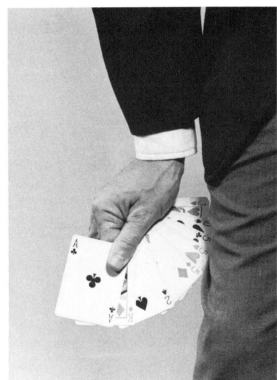

Figure 163

cards, and immediately take the deck in the right hand for the apparent purpose of showing your left hand empty (Figure 161). Do this with just a wave and a turn, a kind of flourish, and then toss the deck back into the left hand, turn toward the front, and drop the right hand to your side.

As the right hand drops to the side, the fingers alter their grip on the cards, as just explained. The hand should look as if you are about to pluck a thread from the leg of your trousers (Figure 162). Look down at your hand, then reach behind your right leg, fan the palmed cards, and bring them into view (Figure 163). Square them up and toss them back onto the deck.

That is only one of several possibilities available to you once you learn the front-palm production. Instead of dropping the hand and producing the cards from the leg, you can reach up and back and produce them from the air. Or you can reach behind your left elbow or under the left side of your coat and produce the fan. For close-up work, productions from the body are safer than from the air, as the appearance of the cards is masked.

Color Changes

Another pretty flourish with cards is the so-called color change, in which the magician changes the face card of the deck by merely passing his hand in front of it. There are dozens of color changes, and they almost all depend on palming. However, palming cards for color changes is a little different from the conventional method. The cards may be held in one of several different ways, and the methods of getting

Figure 164

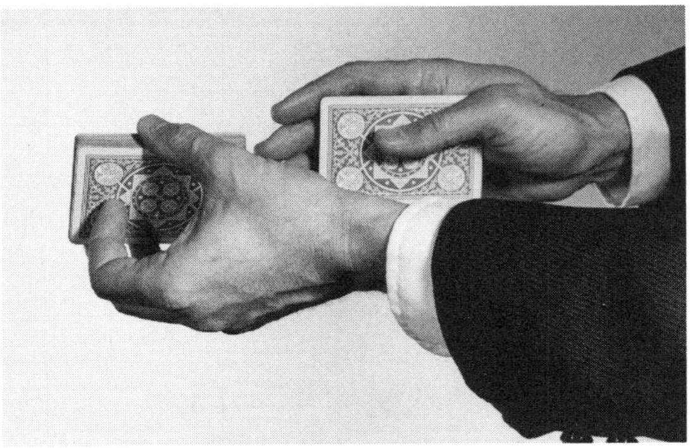

Figure 166

Figure 165

Figure 167

them there are not at all the same. Here are two of the best color changes.

COLOR CHANGE NO. 1

Hold the deck in the left hand, face card to the front, with the thumb on the top long edge and the third, fourth, and fifth fingers on the bottom edge. The forefinger is curled onto the back of the deck. Stand with your right side to the front. Now brush the face card with the right fingers, as if you were flicking dust off the card. The hand moves horizontally, from left to right. Note how the right thumb slides behind the deck as the fingers are extended across the face. At the start of the move, the end of the deck is actually in the crotch of the right thumb.

As the right hand comes across the face of the deck, and the thumb is along the back, extend the left forefinger and with the tip nip off a small packet of cards—about ten to fifteen— from the end of the deck. Push this packet of cards into the right thumb crotch (Figure 164, rear view) and carry it away as the hand moves toward you in the brushing action. The rear view of this steal is shown in Figure 165, the front view in Figure 166.

The right hand returns to the deck immediately, but this time, instead of brushing the face card horizontally, you bring the hand—and palmed cards—*vertically* across the face of the deck from top to bottom and leave the packet of cards there, dropping them onto the tips of the three fingers that support the deck and extend slightly beyond the face (Figure 167). It will appear as if the face card had suddenly and magically changed.

There is a knack to the move, and it takes practice to get it. The right hand must be relaxed as it flicks across the face of the deck. It steals the cards and returns to the deck without hesitation, dropping the cards as it moves downward.

COLOR CHANGE NO. 2

Stand facing three-quarters to the left, holding the deck in the left hand as in the first color change. Grasp the deck with the right hand, low at the ends, between the thumb and forefinger, so the face card can still be seen. Now you must simultaneously address the spectators and do the following move. Say something to get their attention, such as, "How many

Figure 168

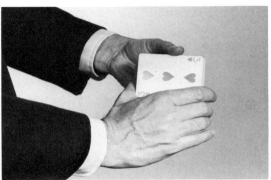

Figure 169

Figure 170

Figure 171

cards in the deck?" As you speak, break off about ten cards with the left thumb at the top edge of the deck, curl the little finger onto the back, and draw these cards downward (Figure 168, side view). The cards are held between the two middle fingers at the face of the packet and the first and fourth fingers at the back of the packet. And as you do this, turn toward the left so your right side is facing front. This all serves as misdirection for the move.

When the packet clears the bottom of the deck, the right second finger can press against its outer edge and hold it against the palm (Figure 169, left hand removed). Do not move the left thumb from the top edge. You now have the packet palmed in the right hand, on edge, with the face card down. You also hold the deck between the forefinger at one end and the inner part of the thumb at the other.

Raise the left hand above the deck and show that it is empty. Then regrasp the deck in the starting position. Move the right hand slightly out and upward, and rest the packet of cards palmed there on the tips of the left fingers. Spread the right fingers, keeping the second finger over the edge of the packet (Figure 170). Then lever the packet upward and onto the face of the deck, and move the hand downward, stroking the ends of the deck with the right thumb and fingers, revealing the changed card (Figure 171).

The gesture of showing the left hand empty is merely a bit of misdirection, to suggest to the audience that there is nothing concealed in either hand. They see the deck held in the right hand and, if you have palmed the cards smoothly, cannot imagine that you have a packet concealed there. Keeping the left thumb on the edge of the deck is the key to palming the cards undetectably.

11 / Fanning Cards

Along with white-tipped wands, rabbits, and top hats, a fan of playing cards has long been a symbol of the magician's art. One of the surest ways to establish that you are a magician is to remove a deck from its case and proceed to make several pretty fans.

In the last chapter we learned how to produce a fan of ten to twenty cards from the palm. Now we'll learn how to fan an entire deck. It's not really difficult, but it requires a certain knack which sometimes takes a while to learn.

For best results, a deck should be specially prepared for fanning, but unfortunately a fanning deck is useless for normal card work. If you want to do an elaborate series of fans in your show, keep a separate deck for the purpose. A new deck will fan well enough, but it loses its fanning ability through use.

To prepare a fanning deck, get a can of zinc stearate talcum powder from the drugstore. Spread a new deck on a terrycloth towel and lightly sprinkle the cards with the powder. Then pick up the four corners of the towel and shake the cards inside, mixing them with the powder. Gather the cards and give them a half-dozen riffle shuffles, to distribute the powder evenly through the deck and to get rid of the excess. Finally, look through the deck and wipe any cards that are caked with powder. Now they are ready for fanning.

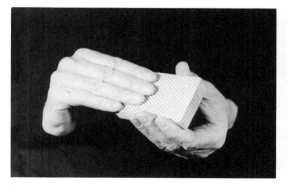

Figure 172

Figure 173

Figure 174

One-Hand Fan

This fan of the entire deck is a carry-over from the palm
production of ten cards explained in the last chapter. The only
difference is that you don't palm the deck. You grasp it with
the first three fingers of the right hand on top and the thumb
underneath. The fingers should be parallel to the sides of the
deck and extend upon its back up to the first joints (Figure
172).

To make a fan, push to the left with your thumb and to the right with your three fingers (Figure 173). As the deck begins to spread, turn the hand in a circular motion, bringing the face toward the front. As the deck approaches maximum spread, the first finger presses downward, completing the fan (Figure 174).

To close the fan, cup the left hand under the left-hand edge and reverse the movement.

The Finger (or Thumb) Fan

The size of this fan can be varied by changing the grip on the deck. Some magicians use a finger to form the fan, others the thumb. It's just a matter of which method suits you best. I prefer the finger, and so the photos show my hands making the fan in this fashion.

Hold the deck vertically in the left hand, with the first two fingers across the front lower half of the deck and the thumb across the back (Figure 175). The fingers are parallel to the *ends* of the deck this time; but pressure is exerted with only the tips.

To make the fan, press the right forefinger, second finger, or thumb against the upper left side of the deck about an inch from the top corner, and spread the cards in an arc to the right (Figure 176). This is where the knack comes in. You must find just the proper combination of right-finger pressure with a slight pull of the *left forefinger*—together they spread the deck. The left finger gives the fan the needed spread to

Figure 175

Figure 176

Figure 177

the left while the right finger (or thumb) spreads it to the right. The completed fan is shown in Figure 177.

Experiment with the placement of the right finger on the upper corner of the deck. Depending on the condition of the deck, you may have to vary it a half-inch or so in either direction.

When you have learned to make the basic finger fan, experiment with different grips. By gripping the deck higher, the size of the fan can be reduced. You can even do an impromptu diminishing card routine by gradually raising your

Figure 178   Figure 179

grip on the cards on successive fans. Each time they will appear to have shrunk a little more.

This fan can be closed by bringing the right forefinger in contact with the left edge of the fan and describing an arc with the right hand. A showier method is to close the fan with the left hand alone. This takes a little practice. The left second finger must be extended to exert pressure on the near corner of the fan (Figure 178, arrow), pulling it downward and closing the fan, with the help of the other fingers, so the deck ends up squared in the hand.

The fan can be made with either the fingers or the thumb toward the audience, with the faces or the backs of the cards to the front. Unless you are using a special decorative fanning deck, the faces look best. This fanning deck has four-color backs that enable you to make varicolored fans, as shown in Figure 179.

Reverse Thumb Fan

With this method it is possible to fan a deck so the cards appear to be blank. First do a finger fan showing the indices of the cards, then do a reverse thumb fan; it looks as if you

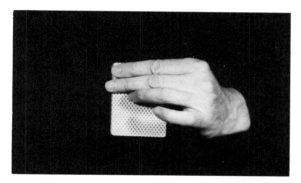

Figure 180

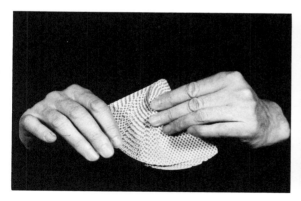

Figure 181

Figure 182

have changed the cards into blanks. The reverse thumb fan is also used with four-color fanning decks to utilize the two colors that can't be shown with the normal finger fan.

Hold the cards vertically in the left hand, with the first two fingers across the top parallel with the end and the thumb across the rear (Figure 180). Now place the ball of the right thumb about a half-inch or so from the lower left corner of the deck and describe an arc upward and around to the left, fanning the cards as you did in the finger fan—but in reverse (Figure 181). Done properly, the fan should be blank. Turn the cards and show the faces to the audience (Figure 182).

Pressure Fan

This is another method of fanning a deck, especially suited to cards that are not in the best condition. This method produces a wider spread and a larger fan. It is often used to fan a deck when asking a spectator to select a card. In any case, it is a showy flourish.

Hold the cards in the left hand as for the finger fan, first two fingers at the bottom and parallel with the end, thumb tip about a half-inch from the right bottom corner. Now grasp the deck with the right hand, first three fingers at the top end and thumb at the bottom. Pivot the deck to the left, into the thumb crotch, at the same time squeezing it between the right thumb and fingers, bending the cards under pressure. Now fan the cards to the right and gradually release the pressure at the same time (Figure 183, side view). The cards will escape from the fingers and form themselves into the fan (Figure 184). This takes practice, but once you get the knack you'll wonder why it took you so long.

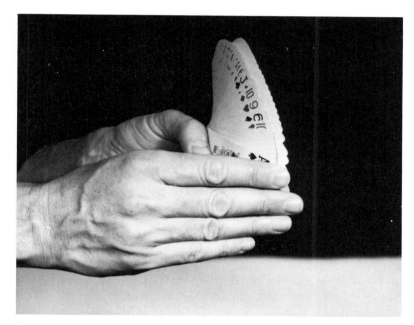

Figure 183

Figure 184

This fan can be shown with faces and thumb toward the front or with faces and fingers front. Of course, if you are using a multicolored fanning deck, you would keep the backs of the cards to the front.

Close the fan by extending the left second finger to the corner and pull down, helping the cards along with the other fingers until the deck is squared in the palm.

Split Fans

This is the showiest flourish of all, not at all hard to do.

Hold the deck in the left hand at the sides, between the thumb and last three fingers, with the forefinger curled against the face card. Grasp the deck at the ends with the right thumb and fingers, and with the thumb split off half the deck and slide it forward half an inch (Figure 185, side view). Move the right thumb forward and curl the right fingers around the ends of the cards so you can grip both packets between the fingers and thumb. At the same time, bend the

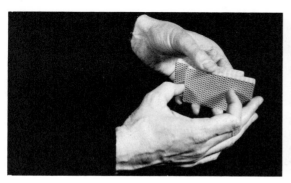

Figure 185

Figure 186

right wrist inward and bring the face card front. Then grasp the front packet, which overlaps the rear packet on the left, between the thumb and first three fingers of the left hand (Figure 186). Split the deck, fanning both packets simultaneously by pushing up with the thumbs and down with the fingers (Figure 187).

Close the fans by reversing the movement and square them in the left hand.

The flourish should be performed with a graceful wave of both fans, outward and back, the two fans melding and closing into one deck again, like two butterflies emerging suddenly from a cocoon and then retreating.

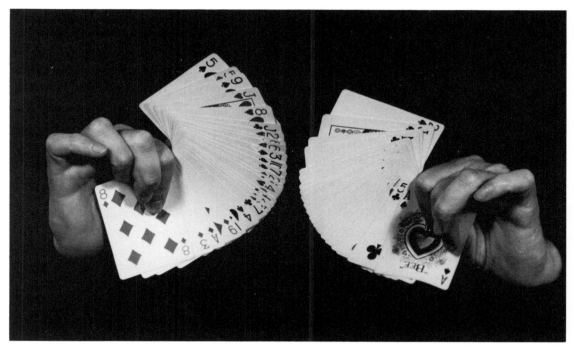

Figure 187

12 / The Cups and Balls

This trick has been performed over the centuries by the magicians of ancient Egypt, Greece, and Rome, the fakirs of India, the sorcerers of China and Japan, and the strolling jugglers of Europe. It is still exhibited by every magician worthy of the name. Houdini said he could not consider a man a magician unless he was adept at the cups and balls.

The equipment for the effect consists of three cups and several balls, but these have assumed different forms in different lands. The cups have been of tin, wood, crockery, or paper, the balls of stone (pebbles), cork, rubber, wood, or wadded cloth. Chinese magicians often used cherries.

A modern outfit, available from magic dealers, consists of three nesting brass or aluminum cups and four wooden balls jacketed in knitted wool.

With only three cups and four balls, a skillful manipulator can perform all sorts of shenanigans. The balls pass from one cup to the other, vanish, penetrate, and eventually change into lemons or other fruits. Conjurors have been known to produce baby chicks as a finale.

The purpose of this chapter is to teach the basic sleights used in cup-and-ball work and to give you an easy routine with a teacup and four balls to get you started. You can use

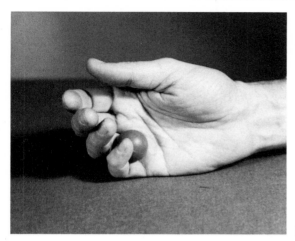

Figure 188

grapes, olives, or foil balls, or you can carve your balls from
bottle corks. The photos show small rubber balls I found in a
Japanese shop in Manhattan.

There are really only three sleights needed to perform
some very mystifying juggles with the cups and balls. One is
our old friend the pass. The second is loading a ball secretly
under a cup. The third is pretending to put a ball under a cup
but palming it instead.

The Pass

The easiest way to palm a small ball is at the base of the
little finger. Just curl the finger inward and hold the ball
lightly in the crook (Figure 188). Once you become accustomed to holding the ball there, you will be able to maneuver
the cups around with ease.

Figure 189

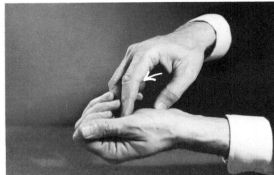

Figure 190

Again, as in coin and spongeball magic, we must devise a way to perform a fake transfer of a ball from one hand to the other. Here is one of the best methods:

Hold the ball in the right hand, between the thumb and first two fingers. Bring the right hand over to the left, turning inward, and with the thumb roll the ball across the fingers (Figure 189) into the curl of the little finger. The left fingers close around the right fingers, where the ball used to be, and the right little finger grips the ball securely (Figure 190, arrow, side view) as the left hand moves away. It's done smoothly and casually, the thumb rolling the ball into the little finger palm and returning immediately to its natural position. The right hand, with the ball palmed, points toward the left, as in other palms, and your gaze is focused on the left hand.

This pass resembles somewhat the pass with a spongeball (page 75). Both are performed in a casual manner, as if the transfer of the ball from hand to hand was the least important part of the trick. Also, both passes occur during the course of a routine with more than one ball and should not be emphasized. The emphasis should be placed on the *disappearance* of the ball, not on the transfer. It should appear to the audience that transferring the ball from right hand to left is simply a matter of convenience.

One way to impart this impression, when doing a complete cups-and-balls routine, is to use a wand. The wand is placed on the table slightly to your right. You then perform the fake transfer as if you needed to have your right hand free to pick up the wand. The transfer of the ball is thus "justified" by the apparent need to pick up the wand with the right hand.

This pass alone will suffice to perform a number of mystifying moves and routines with the cups and balls. In fact, it is preferable to transfer the ball in the same way each time, again to play down the importance of the transfer itself.

Loading a Ball Under a Cup

This is *the* essential move in cups-and-balls magic and should be practiced until it can be performed flawlessly. The move is *not difficult*—let me emphasize this at the start—but the beginner may at first encounter a problem in releasing the ball beneath the cup without telltale finger movements. This is natural and should not discourage you from striving to master this move. Once you learn it, you will have at your command an important tool, the mastery of which will help you in other branches of sleight of hand. There are many effects in magic that require loading an object, large or small, beneath a container of some kind; and if you can learn to do it with a small ball, you can do it with a rabbit.

The ball to be loaded is palmed in the right hand, held as previously explained by the curled little finger. If you are using a teacup, as in the photos, the handle should be pointing outward.

Now, what you are going to pretend to do is reach down, pick up the cup, and show there is nothing beneath it. To satisfy the audience, you need only raise the cup a few inches from the surface of the table. You do not show the audience the inside of the cup, merely the small area of the table under the cup.

Grasp the cup with the thumb and first three fingers, allowing the edge of the hand to rest on the table. The hand should be turned in slightly, so the right heel contacts the table (Figure 191). The little finger, curled in to hold the ball, rests on its edge, the thumb tip contacts the table, and the ball itself may just touch the surface. This initial grip is very important; unless you grasp the cup properly you won't be able to load the ball unobtrusively when you replace it on the table.

In raising the cup, move it slightly back and to the right—a matter of 4 or 5 inches—at the same time tilting the mouth inward (Figure 192). As the hand moves up and back, bend the thumb inward, and also bend the second and third fingers, pivoting the cup on the fulcrum of the pad of the first finger. Note how the right edge of the cup comes over the ball. Holding the cup in this position, lower it to the table (Figure 193), relaxing the little finger's grip on the ball and allowing it to drop beneath the cup. When this is properly done, the hand should be in the same position upon returning the cup as it was when lifting it.

The key to this move is the pivoting of the cup over the ball in the little finger palm as you lift it from the table. All eyes will be on the spot uncovered by the cup, but even if they were focused on the hand it wouldn't matter, for the movement of thumb and fingers that pivots the cup is so slight as to be imperceptible.

You can also raise the cup with the left hand, transfer it to the right hand, replace the cup, and load the ball as just de-

Figure 191

Figure 192

Figure 193

scribed. This method of loading the ball is sometimes used in a routine to vary the moves. It is perhaps a trifle easier, since the right hand can grasp the cup in a position more nearly over the ball when the cup is taken from the other hand than when it is raised from the table.

As you transfer the cup from the left hand to the right, gesture with the left hand at the spot on the table below the cup, as if to say, "Nothing here." This serves to justify the transfer by giving the left hand a task after it relinquishes the cup.

Practice both these methods of loading a ball until they become second nature, until you can raise a cup and load a ball without thinking about it. That's the way you'll have to do it when performing a complete routine with the cups and balls.

The Fake Insertion

There are times in a routine when you must pretend to place a ball under a cup but keep it palmed. The easiest way to accomplish this is to perform the pass, retaining the ball in the right little finger palm, and pretend to hold the ball loosely in your left fist. Pick up the cup with the right hand and pretend to scrape the ball off the palm of the left hand, opening the hand just as the mouth of the cup comes down on it. The left hand is held just above the table and the cup is slid off the palm onto the surface of the table.

Routines with One Cup and Three Balls

Here is a simple routine with one cup and three balls that can be performed anywhere, on the spur of the moment. I often amaze my companions on a picnic with this routine, using the top of a thermos jug and grapes.

EFFECT

The magician shows a teacup and three small balls. The cup is shown to be empty and is placed mouth down on the table.

Figure 194

Picking up one ball in his right hand, he places it in the left hand, from where it vanishes and appears under the cup. This is repeated with the two other balls until all three balls are found under the cup. One ball is then placed in the pocket but returns to join the other two beneath the cup. Finally, all three balls are placed in the pocket and a lemon is discovered under the cup.

PERFORMANCE

Actually, four balls are required, but the audience sees only three. Like many another magic routine, this one uses the principle of "one ahead." The workings of this principle will become clear in a moment.

Even before beginning the trick, get the fourth ball palmed in the left hand. Use the little finger palm as previously explained. Once you have the ball secreted in the left hand, you can gather three others from the fruit bowl, the ground, or your pocket. Show the three balls in your right hand (Figure 194). Now do the utility move explained in the coin section (page 47). This is just a matter of transferring the balls to the left hand, holding one back in the right little finger palm, and showing the two plus the palmed ball in the left hand. The balls are transferred from hand to hand ostensibly to permit a spectator sitting on your left to see them more closely.

"Here are three balls," you say. Show them, transfer them to the left hand (holding back one), show them to the person at your left, and place them on the table. "And a teacup. Nothing under the cup." With the right hand, raise the cup and replace it on the table, loading the palmed ball.

Pick up one of the balls on the table with the right hand, and pretend to transfer it to the left but retain it palmed in the right (Figure 195). Hold your closed left hand over the cup and pretend to toss the "ball" through the top, but don't touch the cup. Then raise the cup and show the ball beneath it (Figure 196).

Replace the cup on the table, loading the palmed ball. Once more, pick up a ball with the right hand, pretend to transfer it to the left but palm it in the right, and "pass" it through the top of the cup. Raise the cup and show two balls. Replace the cup, load the third ball, vanish the last ball on the table, and show three balls under the cup.

If you would like to make more of this one-cup routine, you can finish by loading a lemon or other small fruit under the cup. Here is how to do it.

At the conclusion of the routine above, you raised the cup and showed three balls. The fourth is palmed in your right hand. The lemon is in your right pocket. Replace the cup

Figure 195

Figure 196

on the table slightly to the left and in front of the three balls, loading the fourth ball as you do so.

With the left hand tilt the cup forward and with the right roll two balls under the lip, one at a time, counting, "One ball, two balls . . ." Release the cup, covering the balls, pick up the third ball in the right hand, and place it in your right pocket, saying, "And the third ball in my pocket." (This is an adaptation of the conclusion of the spongeball routine [page 79], as you have probably discerned, so don't follow one with the other.)

"How many balls under the cup?" The spectators will say two. Lift the cup with the right hand and show three balls. Separate one ball from the three by rolling it a few inches to the side with the tip of the left index finger, and lower the cup onto the two balls, loading the ball palmed in your right hand. "Two balls under the cup," you say, "and one in my pocket." Once again, pick up the third ball and drop it in your pocket. Palm the lemon but don't remove your hand from your pocket just yet.

"Now, how many balls under the cup?" Again the spectators will probably guess two. This time raise the cup with the left hand and show three balls. As the audience's attention is concentrated on the balls, remove your right hand from your pocket and bring the cup down into the hand so it covers the lemon.

Figure 197

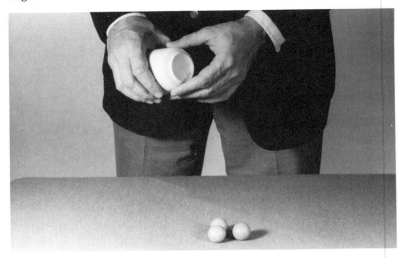

Figure 198

The loading of the lemon must be perfectly timed. Let's go back a moment and rehearse it again, as there are a few details that you should understand.

The left hand raises the cup to reveal the three balls, and a split second later the right hand comes out of the pocket with the fruit, palm turned *toward* the body (Figure 197, hand turned to show lemon). As the hand comes from the pocket, the left hand comes down and across to meet it. The right hand grasps the cup, the thumb and first finger encircling the mouth (Figure 198). This brings the mouth directly over the lemon. Now turn your hand slightly *downward,* pointing the bottom of the cup toward the floor, and allow the lemon to fall *into* the cup. As you feel the lemon fall, bend the little finger inward so it extends across the mouth of the cup, and set the cup on the table. The little finger prevents the lemon from falling out of the cup before the lip touches the table; at the last moment, withdraw the little finger and place the cup to the side of the three balls.

You now have the cup on the table with a lemon beneath it and three balls close by. Pick up the balls in the left hand, one by one, and drop them into the right hand, counting as before, "One ball, two balls, three balls. . . . This time I'll put them all in my pocket. Now how many balls do you think are under the cup?" Regardless of the answer, lift the cup, show the lemon, and take a bow.

When you have learned to pass and load small balls and have mastered this one-cup routine, I suggest that you buy a set of cups and balls from a magic dealer and a booklet entitled *Dai Vernon's Routine with the Cups and Balls,* also available at any magic store. This is perhaps the finest cups-and-balls routine ever created and is well worth the practice required to learn it.

13 / Thimble Magic

Put a thimble on the tip of your right forefinger. Now bend the finger into the palm. Notice where the thimble ends up? In the perfect position for palming it in the crotch of the thumb. Give you any ideas?

Basic thimble manipulation relies almost completely on the thumb palm. Learn this sleight and you can perform a pretty sequence of vanishes with one thimble that is among the most mystifying in magic. These vanishes are ideal for close-up work, especially impromptu, since next to a coin a thimble is about the easiest prop to carry in your pocket. Thimble manipulation is also performed on the stage, but with oversize thimbles. The magician produces one thimble at a time on the tips of his fingers, until all fingers are capped with thimbles.

For basic close-up work, ordinary dime-store thimbles are perfectly suitable. The thimble should be of a size to fit your forefinger loosely enough so it comes off easily in the thumb crotch, but not so loose that it flies off your finger when you bring it out of the thumb palm for reproduction. Experiment with a few sizes until you find the one that suits you.

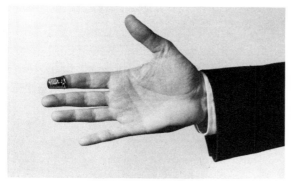

Figure 199

Figure 200

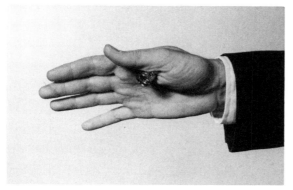

Figure 201

The Thumb Palm

You don't have to be able to thumb palm a thimble terribly quickly to perform several good vanishes, but naturally the more speed you can develop, the better. At first, strive only to hit the target—the thumb crotch—every time and leave the thimble there. Then learn to pick it up smoothly without losing it.

The thumb palm is executed by bending the forefinger into the thumb crotch and removing the thimble by the pressure of the thumb against the side of the hand, as shown in Figures 199, 200, and 201. Carry a thimble around with you and just thumb palm it a few hundred times a day until it becomes easy. Your muscles will stretch and you'll gain speed with practice.

Here are a few ways to vanish a thimble using the thumb palm. As with coins and balls, the vanish is done as a pass, the thimble apparently being transferred from the tip of the forefinger to the palm of the other hand. The thimble can also be vanished by pretending to toss it into the air, thumb palming it with the back of the hand toward the audience.

Vanish No. 1

This is a good vanish to start with because you don't have to thumb palm rapidly to learn it.

The thimble, as always, is on the tip of the right forefinger. Standing with your right side toward the audience, lay the forefinger on the palm of the left hand and close the fingers of that hand on the thimble, one by one, starting with the pinky (Figure 202). As the last finger—the forefinger—closes on the thimble, turn the left hand forward, slowly, its back toward the audience, leaving the thimble on the forefinger but shielding the finger and thimble. At the very moment that the left hand covers the forefinger, thumb palm the thimble (Figure 203, rear view). Immediately bring the right hand in front of the left and rub the back of the left fist with the now empty right forefinger. Turn the left hand over again, fingers toward

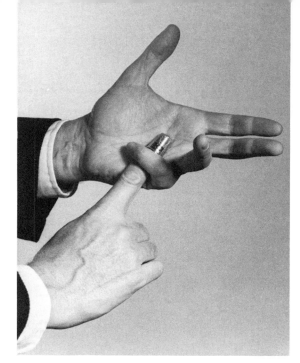

Figure 202

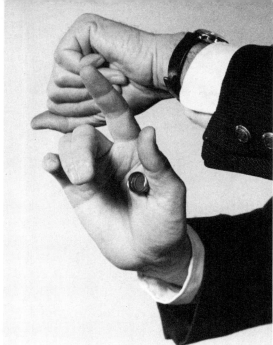

Figure 203

the front but still closed, and give the audience a second to digest the transfer. Then open the left hand, with a slight upward toss or rubbing motion, and show that the thimble has vanished.

My favorite recovery after a thimble vanish is to move the right hand up the forearm behind the elbow, get the thimble from the thumb palm onto the tip of the forefinger, and then pull the hand straight down, exposing the finger, now re-capped with the thimble.

This vanish and recovery should be done slowly, like a slow-motion movie. Note that in both the vanish and recovery the right hand is shielded, allowing ample time to thumb palm and recover. Don't hesitate to call attention to the fact that you are performing the transfer slowly so the audience "can follow more easily."

Vanish No. 2

Whereas the thumb palm in the foregoing vanish is masked by the other hand, here it is masked by a large movement of the right hand itself.

Begin this vanish in the same way as no. 1, standing with your right side toward the audience. Lay the right forefinger, thimble capped, on the left hand, and close the fingers one by one. Then pull the finger out of the fist and drop the hand straight down, thumb palming the thimble. The hand should fall quickly, but allow gravity to pull it down, so it falls limply. Let the right hand fall to your side, but raise it immediately, and point at the left fist for a second before opening the hand and showing that the thimble has vanished.

The long sweep of the right hand covers the thumb palm, and therefore the hand does not have to move downward at great speed. Just let it fall of its own weight, thumb palming the thimble as it drops.

Another effective recovery is to reach behind the open left hand and recover the thumb-palmed thimble on the right forefinger. Then move the left hand upward, exposing the thimble on the finger.

Vanish No. 3

Here again we find a way to mask the actual thumb palming of the thimble and at the same time add a small touch by

Figure 204

giving the audience a glimpse of the thimble in the hand at the very last moment.

Stand facing front this time, and lay the thimble-capped right forefinger on the palm of the left hand. Bring both hands in front of the body, the forefinger encased in the left fist, with the opening of the fist toward the audience. Push the forefinger deeply into the fist until the thimble protrudes a bit in front (Figure 204) and call attention to it. Say something like "You can even *see* the thimble in the fist." Now withdraw the right hand straight backward, toward the body, thumb palming the thimble while the hand is still masked by the left fist; then swing the hands to the left, showing the back of the right hand and the front of the left fist. Vanish as usual and recover from the elbow or behind the left hand.

Vanish No. 4

This vanish is also a pass, but the thimble is not thumb palmed. Instead it is removed from the forefinger with the second finger and thumb and held there. The pass is quite simple to learn.

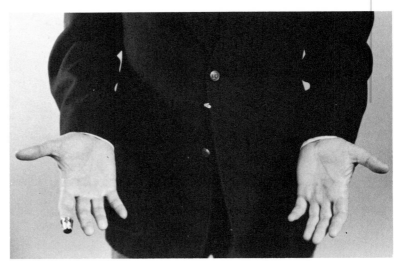

Figure 205

Stand facing front with both hands open, palms up. Display the thimble on the right forefinger, which should be pointing slightly toward the floor (Figure 205). Bring the right hand over to the left, describing an arc of about 18 inches. En route the thumb and second finger grasp the thimble, removing it from the forefinger (Figure 206). When the back of the hand is toward the audience, the thimble, held behind the palm, is invisible. Quickly enclose the forefinger with the left fingers (Figure 207, rear view) and pretend to remove the thimble with the left hand. Then vanish the thimble, as usual, and recover it from the elbow or knee. The recovery of the thimble is especially easy.

Link these four vanishes and you will have a nice little routine for any occasion. Thimble magic proves that you can entertain an audience with the humblest of objects.

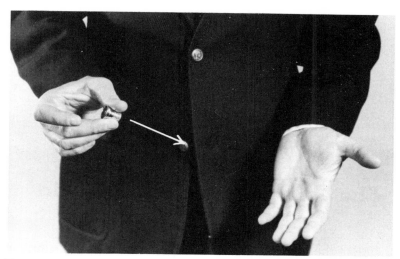

Figure 206

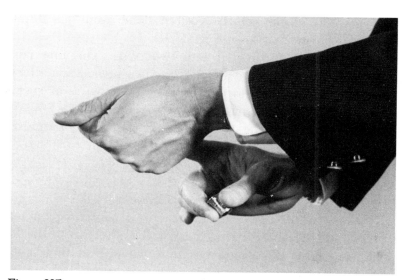

Figure 207

14 / Napkin Magic

The Torn and Restored Napkin

One of the feats a magician is expected to perform is to tear, cut, or otherwise damage something and then magically restore it to its original condition. An appropriate object to use in close-up magic, which is often done around a dinner table, is a paper napkin.

This routine is divided into two parts. The first part, which can be performed alone, is the tearing and restoring of the napkin. The second part is what is known as a "sucker finish," in which the magician pretends to explain how the trick is done, leaving the audience even more perplexed than before.

EFFECT

The magician tears one quarter of a paper napkin into strips, rolls them into a ball, and places the ball in the left fist. Squeezing the torn pieces for a moment, he then opens the ball—and the napkin is seen to be restored.

The magician then offers to explain how the trick is done.

He shows the audience a duplicate napkin ball, which, he says, he switches for the ball of torn pieces. Repeating the trick, he shows how he switched the balls and opens the duplicate. Just when the spectators think they understand the secret, the magician astonishes them by opening the ball of torn pieces which he exchanged for the duplicate, untorn ball. It has been restored as well.

PART 1

PERFORMANCE

First, the simple torn and restored trick. For this you need only two quarters of a standard paper napkin. I use quarters, rather than the whole napkin, because they form smaller balls that are easier to handle.

Prepare the napkins in advance by cutting them with a scissors; otherwise tearing them against the grain will leave ragged edges. The trick looks better when you use a perfect square of paper. Determine which way the grain of the napkin runs, and make a couple of small tears at the edge of one to denote where to start tearing. This way you'll be able to tear the napkin into neat strips.

Of course, if you have to perform on the spur of the moment, just tear the napkin into quarters as best you can, ragged edges or no.

One quarter-napkin should be rolled into a ball and kept in your pocket. Before starting, secretly remove the ball from your pocket and drop it into your lap. (You must be seated at a table to perform this trick.)

Remove the other quarter-napkin from your pocket and display it, holding it at the two top corners. Slowly and deliberately tear the napkin into strips (Figure 208) and then

Figure 208

Figure 209

Figure 210

bunch the strips into a ball. Allow the audience to observe that your hands are empty.

Holding the ball between the tips of the fingers of both hands, a few inches above the surface of the table and a few inches from the edge, mold it slowly before the eyes of the spectators, this way and that, all the while showing your hands empty (Figure 209). Then separate your hands and allow the ball to fall to the table (Figure 210). As the ball falls, drop your right hand to the edge of the table *and your left hand into your lap*. Your eyes are on the ball, and you are pattering along these lines: "Here is a napkin torn beyond

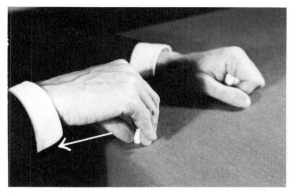

Figure 211   Figure 212

repair. Although I've heard of magicians being able to restore damaged objects, I've never really believed it possible. One magician I've heard of would take a ball of torn pieces, like this one, and hold it for a moment in his hand . . ."

During the foregoing patter, you palm the lapped ball in the left hand and casually bring the hand to the edge of the table, where it rests slightly to the left of the ball. Grasp the ball with the fingers of the right hand, covering it completely, and slide the fingertips (and the ball) along the table toward the edge (Figure 211, rear view). As the fingertips come off the edge, allow the ball to drop into your lap, and bring the hand upright, fingers bunched as if holding the ball and pointing toward the ceiling. Hold this pose for a split second, and then pretend to deposit the "torn pieces" in the left hand. The left turns over to meet the right (Figure 212, rear view). The fingers close at once, and the hand remains closed, on the table, for a few seconds, while you complete your patter.

At the appropriate moment, open the left hand, hold the ball in front of you between the fingers of both hands, and slowly, slowly open it and show that it is restored (Figure 213).

We have seen the lapping move already in the coins

Figure 213

through the table (page 56). It is a most deceptive sleight. But it must not be rushed. It must be done in a natural rhythm. The most important part of the move is the raising of the right hand to a vertical position, *as if you were actually showing the audience the ball*. What they see is just your fingers, but they *think* they see the ball. Hold that position for a second, fearlessly, and then bring the right hand down to the left hand and pretend to deposit the nonexistent ball in the palm that actually contains the duplicate.

PART 2

If you would like to conclude this routine with the "sucker" explanation, at the start you must have two more quarter-napkins, balled up, in your right pocket and another quarter-sheet on the table.

Tell the audience that you are going to show them how to do the trick, and reach into your pocket and palm one ball and bring out the other at the fingertips. Drop the visible ball onto the table, and as it rolls slightly forward, allow the right hand to fall to the edge of the table and drop the palmed ball into your lap.

Figure 214

As you drop the ball onto the table, explain that "naturally the trick depends on having a duplicate ball which I switch for the ball of torn pieces. I keep the duplicate palmed in the right hand." So saying, pick up the ball and conceal it in your hand in a not-too-expert palm.

Although you convinced the audience the first time that your hands were empty, thus allaying any suspicion of a duplicate ball, they will suppose they were unobservant and accept your explanation.

Proceed to tear the other quarter-napkin into strips (Figure 214) and roll them into a ball. Hold the ball, as before, between the fingers of both hands, but keep the palmed ball out of sight. Then visibly switch the two balls, explaining in your most persuasive manner exactly what you are doing. Open the duplicate ball and show that of course the napkin is "restored." There will be a feeling of anticlimax at this moment; just drop the ball of torn pieces on the table and gaze complacently at the audience, as if you expected to be commended for revealing such a guarded secret.

Allow your right hand to fall naturally into your lap and palm the other ball, but not in the usual way; hold it behind the first joints of the fingers, with the thumb. Pick up the "re-

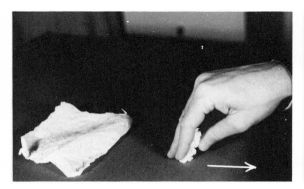

Figure 215

Figure 216

Figure 217

stored" napkin with the left hand and move it slightly to the left, using this move to cover the return of the right hand to the edge of the table.

"Of course," you say, "a *real* magician wouldn't need a duplicate ball." And as you speak, bring the right fingers down on the ball of torn strips, slide it toward you (Figure 215), off the edge of the table into your lap, and bring the palmed ball to the fingertips (Figure 216). (This also is identical to a coin move in the coins through the table.) "He should be able to restore a torn napkin by simply blowing on it."

Hold the napkin in front of you, blow your most magical breath, open the ball, and show that it is restored (Figure 217).

The Four Paper Balls and Two Napkins

This routine is one version of an old classic that has been done with many different objects. In every instance the plot of the trick involves the passage of the objects—coins, cards, balls—from one place to another. The objects may pass from one hat to another, from under one corner of a newspaper or napkin to another, or, as here, from under one napkin to another.

EFFECT

The magician shows four paper balls, which he places on the table to form a square, and two cloth napkins. He places each napkin over a paper ball, leaving two exposed. He then picks up one paper ball and taps it under the table, directly below one of the napkins. He raises the napkin, and the paper ball is seen to have passed up through the table and joined the other ball already there. In the same manner, the magician causes the other two balls to pass, until all four balls have gathered under one napkin.

PERFORMANCE

You need two cloth dinner napkins and four small paper balls, about a quarter-inch in diameter. The napkins should be folded, as dinner napkins usually are, into fourths. The balls can be rolled from a scrap of paper napkin left over from the torn and restored trick or borrowed from the host. Wet them slightly with saliva as you roll them so they'll compress snugly. You should be sitting at a table to perform this trick.

Place the balls on the table about a foot apart to form a square. Two balls should be about 6 inches from the edge of the table.

Hold the napkins on your outstretched palms (Figure 218) and patter as follows: "For this little trick we use four paper balls and two napkins. We're going to cover two paper balls and leave two exposed. It really doesn't matter which ones. Suppose we cover this ball"—the right-hand, near one—"with one napkin . . ."

As you speak, lower your right hand with the napkin draped across the palm and cover the near right ball (Figure 219), keeping your hand palm up. Clip the ball between the second and third fingers. Withdraw the hand from beneath the napkin and quickly take hold of the corner of the napkin in the left hand (Figure 220), as if you were giving that hand a little assistance, saying, ". . . and we'll cover"—pause—"this

Figure 218

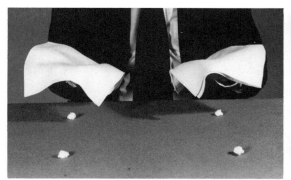

Figure 219

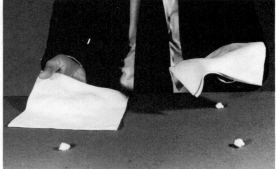

ball with the other napkin." Using both hands, with a dainty gesture drop the left-hand napkin on the left near ball, releasing the finger-clipped ball under the napkin (Figure 221).

This is a bold move, but you can get away with it. The secret is in the slight hesitation before covering the left-hand ball, coupled with a somewhat distracted air. This pause, as if you are deciding which ball to cover, justifies the rather dubious use of two hands on the left-hand napkin. Don't belabor the pause and the indecision; just hesitate for a split second, long enough to absent-mindedly bring up the right hand to the napkin while looking at the three exposed balls. Then pretend to decide on the ball at your near left and drop the napkin (and the finger-clipped ball).

You now have two balls under the napkin at the left and none under the napkin at the right. The most important part of the trick is done.

Review the situation for the audience: "Now we can begin. We have a ball under the napkin to my right and a ball under the napkin to my left. And two balls are visible."

Pick up one of the exposed balls with the right thumb and

Figure 220

Figure 221

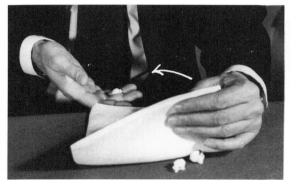

Figure 222

Figure 223

second finger, and bring it under the table below the left-hand napkin. As soon as the ball is out of sight, roll it between the second and third fingertips. Knock on the underside of the table. Grasp the far corner of the napkin with the left hand and turn it back toward the edge of the table—to reveal two balls. This is shown in Figure 222, in which the right hand has been raised above the table edge.

The left hand continues toward your body, turning the napkin over and onto the right hand, which comes directly under the napkin and takes it with the thumb above and fingers below (Figure 223). The left hand then grasps the far corner of the napkin diagonally across from the right hand, and both hands drop it over the two balls, releasing the third from the finger clip beneath the napkin.

Pick up the other exposed ball, place it under the table as before, tap, peel back the napkin and show three balls, and load the last ball. Now all four balls are under the left-hand napkin, but the audience thinks there is one ball under the napkin at the right.

Grasp the edge of this napkin with the left hand, turn it up slightly, just enough to slip the right fingers underneath, remove them bunched at the tips *as if they held a ball,* and put the hand under the table, beneath the left-hand napkin, say-ing, "And now the fourth ball passes up through the table like the others." Tap the table, remove the napkin (in exactly the same way), and show all four balls under the napkin.

15 / Silk Magic

The Vanishing Silk

Every magician dreams of the ultimate vanish. In this dream he picks up any object of his choosing, makes a magical pass, and—poof!—the object disappears.

One of the cleanest vanishes in magicdom can be done with a handkerchief pull and a silk handkerchief. For those unacquainted with this old gimmick, a handkerchief pull is a small cup attached to an elastic, the end of which is secured under the coat. The cup is concealed in the hand and the silk is tucked into the cup, which is then released and allowed to fly beneath the coat. Presto! A total vanish.

The only trouble with the handkerchief pull is that you have to wear a coat to use it. Moreover, you have to get the pull into your hand unobserved, which may not be so easy under the conditions of close-up performing.

Here is a more interesting way to vanish a silk. The gimmick for this vanish is the little hair curler described in the spongeball routine (page 79). A lightweight, 12-inch silk, sold by magic dealers, just fits into this small tube. Remember to cover one end with an adhesive bandage.

Figure 224

The tube can be in your left pants pocket and the silk in your right, or the tube can be clipped under your coat with a bobby pin, or it can be in your left coat pocket. Let's say the tube is in your left pants pocket, the silk in your right pants pocket. Reach into both pockets, as if you don't remember where you put the silk, and come out with the silk in the right hand and the gimmick finger palmed in the left, open end up.

Hold the silk at the corner, between thumb and forefinger, forearm to the side so the hand can be seen empty, and patter as follows: "Have you noticed how suspicious people are getting? They don't believe politicians any more. They don't even believe magicians. For example, if I tuck a silk into my hand . . ."

Make a fist around the gimmick and tuck the silk into the opening, using the first and second fingers of the right hand, alternately (Figure 224). When the silk is completely con-

Figure 225

cealed in the fist, drop your right hand and slip it into your right pants pocket for a moment, and withdraw it.

Continue pattering: ". . . and say the magic word *abracadabra . . .*" Stop, look at the audience as if you heard someone speak, and say, "What's that? I put it in my pocket? You see what I mean? Suspicion. As a matter of fact, the silk is still in my hand."

Reach into your fist with the thumb and second finger, nip the corner of the silk, and withdraw it so that just a couple of inches protrude (Figure 225). Hold the hand at about chest height, knuckles toward the ceiling.

"That's what I mean. If I tuck a silk into my hand"—retuck the corner into the fist—"and innocently slip my hand into my pocket . . ."

When you retuck the silk into the gimmick, give it a couple of last pokes with the first and second fingers, insert the thumb, and grasp the edge of the gimmick between the sec-

Figure 226   Figure 227

ond finger and thumb. (This is the spongeball vanish described on page 79.) Pull the gimmick straight out and turn the left hand, fingers to the front (Figure 226). Bend the gimmick into the right palm on the tip of the second finger and thrust your hand into your pocket with the words ". . . innocently slip my hand into my pocket . . ." As soon as the hand enters the pocket, finger palm the gimmick, pinch the bottom of the pocket between thumb and forefinger, and turn it inside out, keeping the back of your hand toward the audience (Figure 227), saying, ". . . people think I've stolen the silk . . . which is untrue, because, as you can see, my pocket is empty . . ." Stuff the pocket back and leave the gimmick, withdrawing your hand immediately.

Pause a beat and continue. "Of course, if I really want to make the silk disappear, all I have to do is blow on my fist— and it vanishes." Open your left hand slowly and show that the silk has disappeared.

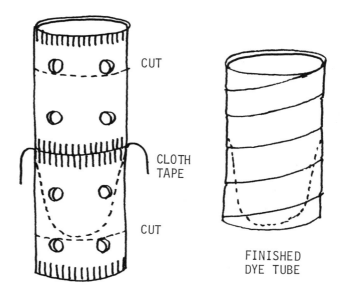

CUT

CLOTH
TAPE

CUT

FINISHED
DYE TUBE

Figure 228

The Color-Changing Silk

With two short hair curlers, or a long one cut into two 1-inch sections, you can not only vanish a silk handkerchief but first change its color. In addition to the two curlers, you'll need a length of ⅝-inch nonadhesive cloth tape and a roll of tan (or other fleshlike tone) adhesive cloth tape. As shown in Figure 228, the nonadhesive tape is sandwiched between the two curlers so that it loops within, and all is held in place

Figure 229

Figure 230

by a few turns of the tan adhesive. Tan is close enough to skin color to camouflage the gimmick. You have just made what is known as a dye tube.

Tuck a blue silk handkerchief into the tube (Figure 229) and put it in your right pants pocket. Put a white silk in your left pants pocket. (These colors are, of course, arbitrary. For photographic purposes we used white and blue.)

Now begin as with the vanishing silk, except in reverse— that is, you come out with the white silk in your left hand and the tube in your right, finger palmed with the *open* end toward the *rear*, the length of the tube parallel with the fingers (Figure 230).

Show the white silk toward your left and wave it up and down a few times, also showing that your left hand is empty. Transfer the silk to the right hand, taking it between the thumb and forefinger. Hold it in front of your body, with the

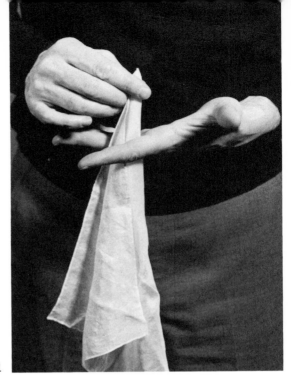

Figure 231

back of the right hand toward the audience, being sure the tube is well concealed. Now advance the left hand toward the silk, palm up, and clip it between the first and second fingers, just below the right fingers (Figure 231). It's as if your fingers were a pair of scissors and you wanted to cut the silk about a half-inch below where it is held by the right thumb and forefinger. This will bring the open left palm immediately below the tube. Release the tube from the right finger palm and it will fall into the left palm, *across* the fingers rather than parallel with them (Figure 232, side view). And now stroke the silk between the first and second fingers, moving the left hand down and the right hand up (Figure 233, side view). You have secretly transferred the tube from the right hand to the left hand while leading the audience to believe that both hands are empty.

The tube is in the left hand, with the open end facing

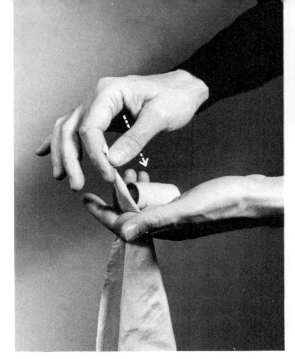

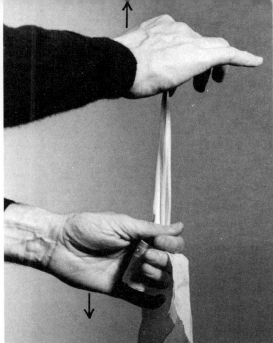

Figure 232   Figure 233

down—this is very important. Face slightly toward your right, and begin tucking the white silk into the tube. The white silk will of course push the blue silk out the bottom of the tube. Allow the corner of the blue silk to emerge from the bottom of your hand, but control its emergence to coincide with the entrance and disappearance within your hand of the white silk (Figure 234). At the same time, turn your body slowly toward the left. It must look as if it is the same silk passing through your hand, only that part above your hand is a different color from that part below.

Just before all the blue silk emerges from the fist, nip the corner with the left pinky and prevent it from falling to the floor. You are facing toward the left now. Tuck the white silk tightly into the tube, and then grasp the tube between the thumb and second finger and steal it, just as in the vanishing silk and the spongeball routine (Figure 235, side view).

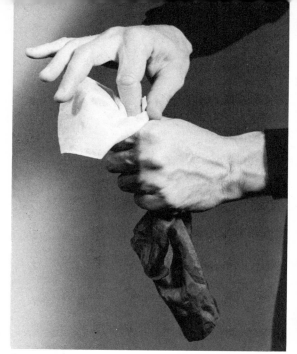

Figure 234

Figure 235

Open your left hand and grasp the blue silk between the thumb and forefinger, showing that it has changed color.

Immediately transfer the blue silk to the right hand, taking it between the forefinger and thumb but keeping the back of the hand toward the audience to conceal the tube, which is on the tip of the second finger, pressed into the palm. At the same time, turn so you are facing front. Bring the left hand up to stroke the silk, but not the way you did it before. This time, the back of the hand faces the audience and the stroke begins just above the right fingers. This allows the second finger to lever the tube into the left palm (Figure 236, side view). Close your fist on it and continue the stroke, whipping the silk upward with the right hand (Figure 237).

You now have the tube back in the left hand, having shown both hands empty, and with the opening facing up.

Figure 236

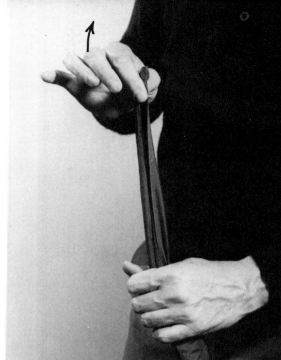

Figure 237

You can conclude in either of two ways. You can perform the vanishing handkerchief, using the dye tube like the shorter hair curler, by tucking the blue silk into the open end of the tube, which is now facing *up*. Or you can pocket the silk and tube. Here is how to accomplish the latter.

You have the blue silk in the right hand, held between the forefinger and thumb in front of the body. You are facing front. Grasp the silk, about 4 inches below the right fingers, in the left thumb crotch, and carry it away, to the left, turning your left hand toward the audience. The silk will mask the tube (Figure 238).

Now grasp the bottom corner of the silk between the right thumb and forefinger and stretch it taut. Turn the left hand over, grasp the silk between the thumb and forefinger, extract the last three fingers from the fold, turn the hand face front, and grasp the silk again with these fingers (Figure

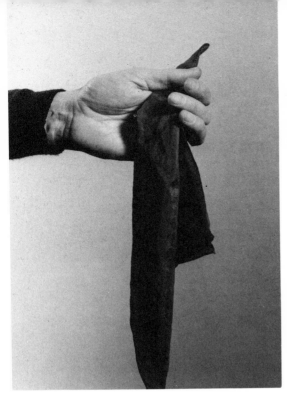

Figure 238

Figure 239

239). Fold all the silk this way, tuck the bottom corner into the hand, and slip the silk into your left pocket. It looks as if you have just folded up the silk, with a flourish, in order to pocket it.

ALTERNATE METHOD

Here is another way to make the color change. You may find that it suits your style and rhythm better than the first method.

The routine begins in the same way: the tube is transferred from the right hand to the left hand. Tuck the white silk into the tube in exactly the same way, but keep the left little finger clamped tightly over the mouth so the blue silk cannot emerge. Tuck the white silk all the way into the tube and poke it in with the right first and second fingers, alternately.

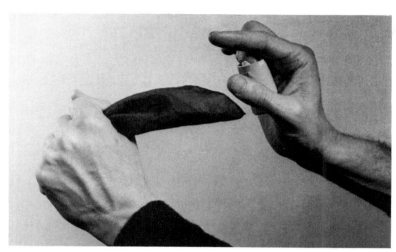

Figure 240

By the time the silk is completely into the tube, you should be standing with your right side toward the audience. Now steal the tube exactly as for the spongeball or handkerchief vanish. Pull it straight out. It will be masked by the right hand and won't be seen. Pulling the tube out also pulls part of the blue silk from the fist and it will flash into view (Figure 240, side view). To the audience it appears that you have tucked a white silk into your hand, then pulled a corner of the silk out of the hand—and it changed color. The change is instantaneous. Open the left hand and show the silk, grasping it by the corner between the thumb and forefinger and giving it a few shakes. The left hand is seen to be empty; the change is inexplicable.

Conclude the routine as before, by transferring the tube back to the left hand and performing the vanishing silk, or by just pocketing silk and tube.

16 / The Cut and Restored Ribbon

Like the vanishing handkerchief, a cut and restored trick—rope or ribbon—must have a humorous twist to be really entertaining. Here is a routine with ribbon that follows up on the first restoration with an amusing bit of audience participation and a fake "explanation" of the trick, similar to that in the torn and restored napkin (page 188).

EFFECT

The magician shows a length of ribbon and snips it in half with a scissors. He trims the cut ends, waves his hand over the ribbon, and restores it. He then offers to explain the trick and asks a spectator to assist him. He shows two ribbons, of the same length, and asks the spectator to cut them in half. The magician gives the spectator two of the strands and keeps two for himself. He then ties his two strands of ribbon together and instructs the spectator to do likewise with his. Both the magician and the spectator then coil their ribbons into several loops. When the magician uncoils his ribbon, the knot has disappeared; the ribbon is restored. The spectator's ribbon, however, is still in two pieces.

PERFORMANCE

The only requirements for this charming trick are two
pieces of ribbon, one about 48 inches long and the other 4
inches shorter, and a small pair of scissors. Put the ribbons in
different pockets and remember which is which. The scissors
go in the right pocket.

PART 1

Remove the longer ribbon and hold it by one end between
the left forefinger and thumb, the ribbon passing between the
first and second fingers. About 2 inches of ribbon should protrude above the left hand. The left hand should be held at
about chest height, back toward the audience. Grasp the ribbon with the right hand at a point about two-thirds down, and

Figure 241

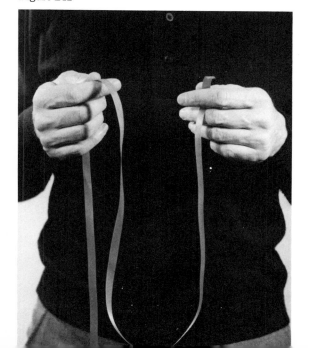

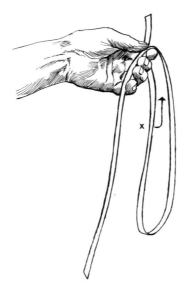

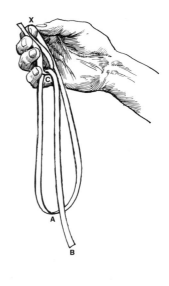

Figure 242   Figure 243

raise the right hand so it is level with the left. You are now in
the position shown in Figure 241.

Drape the loop held in the right hand across the left forefinger and hold it in place with the left thumb. This position is
shown in Figure 242, which is a side view drawn from the
performer's right. You should be holding the ribbon with the
left thumb against the pad of the left forefinger.

Now grasp the ribbon about 2 inches below the left thumb,
between the right forefinger and thumb. This would be at
point X in Figure 242. Raise the right hand, forming a loop.
Turn to the left and clip the short end between the right first
and second fingers while still maintaining the hold on point X
with the forefinger and thumb (as shown in Figure 243). This
will allow you to release your grip on the ribbon with the left
forefinger and thumb, encircle the interlocking loops and the
adjacent strand with the left fingers, regrasp the ribbon as
shown in Figure 244, and release the right-hand hold. The

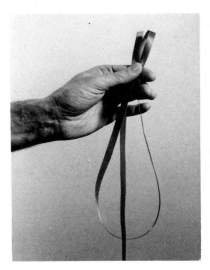

Figure 244

second finger is open in the photo to show a bit of the interlocking loops; it should actually hide them.

This entire operation is done quickly and casually as you turn to the left, the right fingers masking the actual looping of the ribbon. To the audience it should appear as if you merely formed the ribbon into a single loop, part of which protrudes above the left hand and part of which descends below it. In reality you have formed two loops, a large one interlocked with a small one.

If you have followed the instructions carefully, the bottom of the large loop—A in Figure 243—should hang a couple of inches above the end B. Grasp end B in the right hand and give it a gentle pull, just enough to raise the bottom of loop A so it is halfway between the top of loop C and end B.

The most important part of the trick has been done, and the audience doesn't even know yet what you are going to do. You have set up the ribbon in the basic pattern that is used in

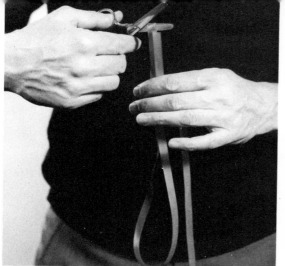

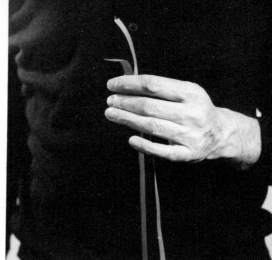

Figure 245

Figure 246

most cut-and-restored tricks. With the ribbon looped in this fashion, it is possible to cut it at what appears to be the middle but is actually the end. Watch.

Remove the scissors from your pocket and bring the left hand to the front of your body, back toward the audience. Slip the blade into the top loop and cut the ribbon, as shown in Figure 245. There will be three ends protruding above your left forefinger after the cut. One of them is the end of the long strand that loops up from below. Determine which one this is, grasp it between the right thumb and forefinger, pull it free, and allow it to fall. The result, to the audience, will look like Figure 246 but actually will resemble Figure 247. As you can see in Figure 246, it looks as though you were holding two long strands of ribbon in your left hand. The audience sees two short ends protruding above the fingers and two long ends descending below. The real state of affairs is shown in Figure 247: a short strand is looped around a long strand, the join being concealed by the fingers.

Now you must tie the small strand around the long strand and give the impression that you are tying together the two ends of the nonexistent long strands. To make this look real, wind one end of the short strand once around the long strand,

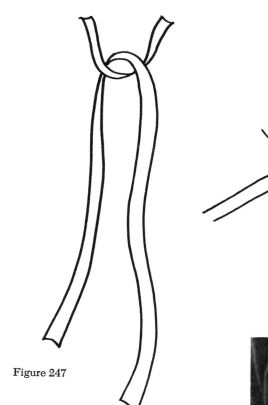

Figure 247

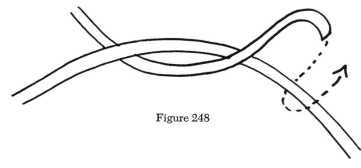

Figure 248

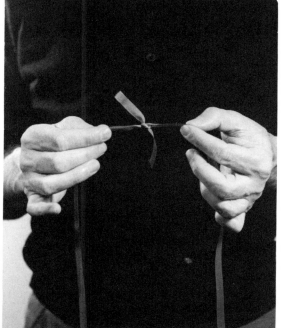

Figure 249

as in Figure 248, before tying an overhand knot. If you just tie the knot directly, it looks a little suspicious, as people know that it takes a couple of turns to tie a square knot, which you would ordinarily use to join two lengths of ribbon. The fingers of both hands mask the knot tying. Don't pull the knot too tight. You have arrived at the point shown in Figure 249. Trim the ends of the knot and, holding the end of the ribbon in the left hand, let it dangle.

To all appearances, you have a length of ribbon composed of two equal strands tied together. In reality you have one long strand of ribbon with a small strand, about 4 inches long, tied around its center. You are still holding the scissors in the right hand. Don't put them away.

Grasp the ribbon with the right hand, just below the left, and slide the hand down to the knot. Pick up the ribbon at this point and coil it in the left hand. It should look as though you placed the knot in the left hand, but you don't—you slide it along the ribbon, concealing it in the right hand (Figure 250, arrow), as you continue coiling the ribbon into the left hand, sliding the knot along and finally slipping it off the end (Figure 251, rear view). As you display the coiled ribbon in the left hand, pocket the scissors (and the knot).

After the proper build-up (see patter, following), grasp an end of the ribbon in the right hand, release the coils in the left hand, and allow the ribbon to fall—restored!

I suggested the patter for this routine in the Introduction to this book, as an example of how certain associations can produce a patter line. Here it is in a fuller form:

"Do you have trouble wrapping Christmas gifts? I do. This is what usually happens. I get the gift all wrapped in pretty paper, then I try to tie it in a red ribbon and finish with a bow. [Here you make the loop for cutting.] And when I clip the ends of the bow, my scissors slip and I cut the loop. Then

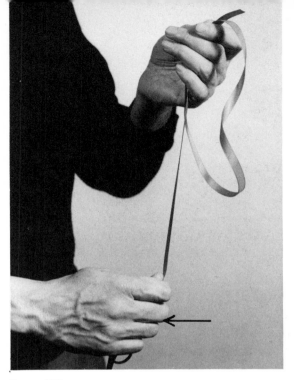

Figure 250   Figure 251

I have to start over again. If I'm low on ribbon I tie the two pieces together . . . and clip the end of the knot so it will look neat. But this doesn't look too good. Then I remember that I'm a magician, and I loop the ribbon like this, warm it in my hand, and—presto!—it's all in one piece again."

PART 2

Toss the restored ribbon toward a spectator and allow it to be examined. While the audience is puzzling over the restoration, offer to explain the trick. Remove the other ribbon from your pocket and hold it by one end between the left forefinger and thumb.

Ask for the first ribbon and grasp it between the right first and second fingers. Show both ribbons in this way (Figure 252).

Figure 252

Bring the two hands together, right slightly above the left, and take the left-hand ribbon between the right forefinger and thumb, clipping the right-hand ribbon between the left first and second fingers. Now move the left hand downward, the forefinger sliding between the ribbons, until it reaches the midpoint. Then release the two ends in the right hand and let them hang over the left hand (Figure 253).

At this point invite a member of the audience to assist you. As he is approaching (on your *left* side), and there is a certain diversion, you perform the following key moves.

1. Clip strand *B* firmly between the first and second fingers and insert the left thumb under it (Figure 254).

2. Break the wrist slightly, allowing strand *A* to fall over the forefinger and across strand *B*, which is supported by the second finger and thumb (Figure 255).

3. Close the left third and fourth fingers, gripping the doubled strands of ribbon, and then enclose the entire join inside the left hand (Figure 256).

This operation takes no more than two seconds. The result is that the two strands of ribbon are now looped together. To the audience it looks as if you are still holding the two separate strands in your left hand. Two strands emerge from one side, two from the other.

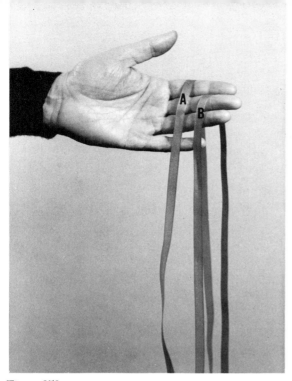

Figure 253

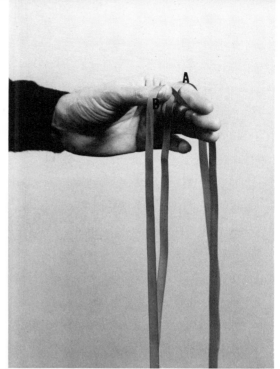

Figure 254

Figure 255

Figure 256

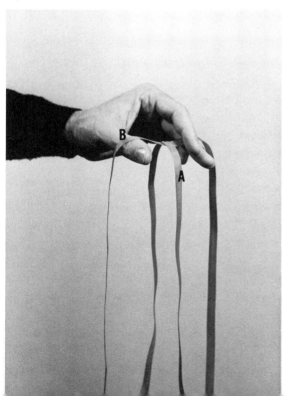

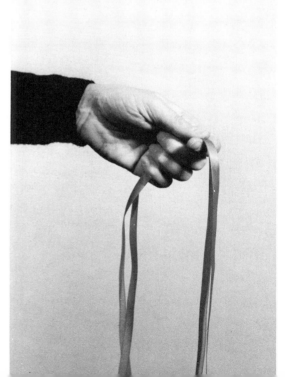

You are now approaching the same situation that you reached in a different way with one ribbon in the first part of the routine. Watch what happens.

Remove the scissors from your pocket, hand them to your spectator-assistant, and ask him to cut the ribbons. To show him where you want him to cut, grasp the two strands that emerge above the left hand about 4 inches from that hand. Ask him to cut between the hands, and give him the two strands in your right hand.

To the audience it looks as if both you and your assistant hold two strands of ribbon. Actually, you have one long strand with a small strand looped around the middle.

Now repeat the same operations as in the first part: tie the small strand around the long strand and coil the ribbon in your hand (palming off the knot). Ask your assistant to do exactly the same thing.

Rub the back of your hand "to create the required warmth" and ask your assistant to do likewise. This, you explain with a wink, is the secret of the trick. *Then uncoil your ribbon and show that it is restored.* When the spectator uncoils his ribbon, it is of course still knotted together. Feign surprise and apologize for having failed to instruct your assistant properly. Again, pocket the palmed knot along with the scissors.

By now you have probably figured out why the first ribbon should be 4 inches longer than the second. When you cut and restore the first ribbon, you'll lose about 4 inches. This will reduce it to the same size as the second ribbon, so you and your assistant will have identical ribbons with which to begin the second part of the trick.

The reason the assistant ought to be directed to your left side is also obvious. When you palm the knot, you should be standing with your *right* side toward the audience.

In Conclusion

This is the end of a book but perhaps it's the beginning of the voyage I mentioned in the Introduction. There are more books awaiting you, hundreds of them, on every branch of magic; and there are marvelous tricks that you can obtain from magic dealers.

Does card magic excite you? There are so many books on the subject that it would take a lifetime to catch up with what's been written while keeping abreast of new developments. The creativity of card magicians is unbelievable.

How about coins? Combining sleight of hand with gimmicked coins and special apparatus can produce fantastic magic.

In fact, you could pick any object in this book and spend months exploring its magical possibilities.

Perhaps you see yourself as a stage magician. There are scores of tricks and illusions that you can purchase and learn to perform. Many magicians work at full-time jobs but augment their income by giving occasional stage shows.

Visit a magic dealer and ask the salesman to demonstrate tricks for you. He is usually an expert magician who can give you a few pointers in the handling of any trick you purchase. A magic shop is also a good place to meet other magicians with whom you can swap tricks and exchange ideas.

Whatever you do, give magic the respect it deserves as an ancient and universal art. Practice diligently. But above all, enjoy yourself!

INDEX